SPRINGBOK FACTORY

SPRINGBOK FACTORY

WHAT IT TAKES TO BE A BOK

L. McGregor

Jonathan Ball Publishers
Johannesburg & Cape Town

First published in 2013 by
JONATHAN BALL PUBLISHERS
a division of Media24 Limited
P O Box 33977
Jeppestown
2043

Paperbook ISBN 978-1-86842-469-6
ebook ISBN 978-1-86842-470-2

Every effort has been made to trace copyright holders and to obtain their permission for the use of copyright material. The publishers apologise for any errors or omissions and would be grateful to be notified of any corrections that should be incorporated in future editions of this book.

Cover by publicide
Design and typesetting by Michelle Staples
Infographics designed by MR Design, Cape Town
Set in 12.5/16.5 pt Gentium
Printed and bound by Paarl Media

Twitter: www.twitter.com/JonathanBallPub
Facebook: www.facebook.com/pages/Jonathan-Ball-Publishers/298034457992
Blog: http://jonathanball.bookslive.co.za/

Contents

fac·to·ry /ˈfakt(ə)rē/ *Noun* **1** a building or buildings where goods are manufactured or assembled. **2** a person, group or institution that produces a great quantity of something.

Introduction

It's been a dreadful tour: three games lost out of four and a whopping great fine for some mysterious misdemeanour. This is the first time Jean de Villiers has faced the local media since the team's return from Australasia and he puts on the usual, masterful performance. I hesitate over the use of the word 'performance', because that implies artifice, a show, when what we get feels utterly authentic. It is a sophisticated narrative that is laid out here, encompassing failure, humiliation and a vision of redemption, with a bit of tragedy thrown in.

First, there is the self-flagellation. De Villiers and Stormers' coach Allister Coetzee scrutinise their team's role in their plight. Last year, the Stormers topped the South African log of the Super Rugby conference. This year, they won't even make the play-offs – poor discipline, too many mistakes, bad decisions. They own up to all of it. In change rooms and team rooms over the past week, emotions have been 'pretty high' and 'a lot of harsh words' have been spoken.

Rugby press conferences can be deadly affairs, leaden with clichés and unconvincing spin. When De Villiers is there, it's different. It always impresses me how skilful he is at this, the part of the game that takes place away from the heat and immediacy of the field. With him, you always feel you are getting the truth. Not the whole truth, because much needs to be kept within the team, but enough to give journalists something real to write about. This is not as easy as it sounds.

This particular conference is taking place in the concrete bunker under the stands at Newlands stadium that does alternating duty as team room and media centre. Next door is the team's change room and, just beyond that, the tunnel through which the Stormers will run onto the field in three days' time to take on the Australian team the Reds. All their energy is now subsumed into this new challenge: another chance to make good. The emotional stakes are ratcheted up by the declaration that the game will be used to raise money for a fallen comrade. Tinus Linee, 43, who played for both the Stormers and the Springboks until 2001, has just been diagnosed with motor neurone disease. The dread letters MND have already been made familiar to the rugby public by the visible attrition the disease has wrought on the once-hulking frame of another former Springbok, Joost van der Westhuizen.

Jean de Villiers tells us that Tinus Linee was his first-ever centre partner and that the pair of them used to travel together from their home town of Paarl to the Stormers' training grounds in Bellville. He holds up his cellphone to demonstrate the epic tackle he once saw Linee inflict on an opposing player. He flips the phone to show what Linee did to the poor bloke. It was a 360-degree somersault. With these vivid verbal pictures, he brings to life a man most of us are not familiar with.

What De Villiers and Coetzee touch on, but don't dwell on – because that falls into the unacceptable category of excuses – is that they have lost a total of 16 members of their team through injury over the past punishing few weeks of Super Rugby. One of them is Springbok lock Andries Bekker, who is now lost for good to South African rugby, as he has taken up a contract in Japan in August. All this has serious implications for the Springbok team of 2013.

In a couple of weeks' time, De Villiers is due to lead the national team in their first Test of the season. Between now and then, though, he has another two Super Rugby games to get through and, as he points out, 'you cannot predict injury'. All the South African teams have been playing Super Rugby week after week for four months now, and Springboks are being felled by injury one after another. The national coach, Heyneke Meyer, must be watching in dismay: how many will be left standing by June, when he has to assemble a team to take on Italy?

I need now to take the reader back a couple of years to an earlier period in Jean de Villiers's – and my own – career. The original idea for this book was that I would follow him and the rest of the Springbok team through the 2011 Rugby World Cup and have a day-to-day diary of a triumphant campaign on the shelves by Christmas. There was little doubt in my mind that the Boks would do well and that they would become the first team ever to retain the Webb Ellis Cup. Like millions of other South Africans, I got caught up in the hype that preceded the team's departure for New Zealand. The national team was, as usual, tasked with much more than just winning a few games. They were a crucial cog in the ongoing struggle for the nirvana of racial reconciliation and the creation of a resilient and united nation. No pressure, then.

The Rugby World Cup has been imbued with special significance ever since 1995, when Nelson Mandela used the one held here to coax white conservatives into accepting the new South Africa. However, the role of rugby in promoting reconciliation was pioneered long before that.

I spent a day in the Robben Island archives, reading, among other things, the constitution of the 'IRB' – not, in this case, the International Rugby Board, the convenor of the Rugby World Cup, but the Island Rugby Board. It is a poignant document – 20 pages of rough, lined paper, covered, schoolbook-style, in brown paper and plastic. Neatly handwritten in blue ballpoint, it is signed off by Steve Tshwete, IRB president, later to be appointed by Mandela to be the first Minister of Sport of a democratic South Africa. This is an extract:

THE ISLAND RUGBY BOARD

Constitution of the IRB
Robben Island
January 30, 1972
Signed by the president, S Tshwete, and secretary, Sedick Isaacs.

Constitution drafted by constitutions committee appointed by the Board in 1969 and approved and signed on Jan 30, 1972.

Aims and objectives:

a) To inculcate the spirit of sportsmanship and co-operation amongst the inmates of Robben Island in all matters of sport and recreation in general.

b) To serve as the sole liaison between the prison authorities and other sporting codes on one hand and the various rugby clubs as set up within the framework of the Board on the other hand.

c) To arrange fixtures for play on a competitive basis and arrange for friendly matches when competitive matches are in progress.

d) To arrange exhibition/variety matches for the purposes of promoting and displaying the game.

e) To elect/select the Ruggerite of the Year on the basis of merit both on and off the field.

f) To register and assist in the formation of clubs by the inmates.

g) To protect the game against abuse in the form of foul play by players on the field and insults and other such obscene language as to bring discredit to the game and the Island Rugby Board.

Springbok Factory

A letter from 1974 showed how the prisoners drew their white captors into the game:

Rugby Referees' Association
Robben Island Prison
ROBBEN ISLAND
12th September 1974

The Rt Hon Chief Warder Gerber
Robben Island Prison

Sir,

I have been instructed by my executive to request you to do us the honour of officiating as referee over a rugby match scheduled for 21st Sept 1974.

We are sure that if you ascede [sic] to our request we stand to gain greatly in rugby refereeing technique.

Yours respectfully in sport,

Secretary, B Mjo

It was while imprisoned on Robben Island that political activists such as Mandela and Tshwete first conceived of the use of rugby as a tool for reconciliation – in this case, between the various political factions who found themselves trapped together on a small island, but also between the black prisoners and the white warders. That rugby for South Africans continues to be much more than a game was underlined by the rapturous sendoff given to the Springboks in 2011 by thousands of fans, both black and white.

It was with this weight of national longing behind them that the Springboks propelled their way through their four pool games. Then came the first of the play-offs, against Australia, on 9 October. Over 80 minutes, all these hopes and dreams slunk away as the Wallabies' score mounted and ours failed to keep up.

It was a shattering defeat, barely comprehensible. I had stayed in the same hotels as the Bok team for several weeks. I had seen at first hand how dedicated and professional were the team on the field and the team behind them. Forty-seven strong, the latter included the team doctor, the physiotherapists and massage therapists, and the logistics and management staff, as well as the phalanx of coaches. Years of preparation had gone into the World Cup campaign – only for it to end in failure.

For me personally, it felt like a disaster. I was left sitting with a 45 000-word manuscript and a memory stick crammed with photographs documenting every step. I had to face the hard fact that no one would want to read about a failed campaign.

All this effort had been in vain.

On the beach at Arniston over the long Christmas holidays, it gnawed away at me. How could I have been so wrong? When I got back to work, I began looking into Springbok records and made a startling discovery. I, along with most South Africans, have always viewed the Springboks as a winning team. After all, in 1995, we had won the first Rugby World Cup we had ever played in. In 2007, we had won it again and, four years later, we entered the 2011 edition as world champions.

But a closer look at the Springboks' win rate reveals that the Boks have in fact won fewer than two thirds of their Test games. Against New Zealand, we have won only 40% of our games.

New Zealand and South Africa share a passion for rugby union, with abundant talent at each country's disposal. Yet, beside us, New Zealand is tiny. It has a population of 4.5 million, compared to our 50 million. Australia, against whom we have won 55.3% of the time, has a different comparative disadvantage: rugby union is only their fourth most popular sport. Football and rugby league are the sports that attract the talent and the fans, followed by cricket.

And yet New Zealand manages to produce rugby union teams that beat ours in 60% of games. Our record against Australia is not much better.

How can this be? We are a proud and passionate rugby nation. We should be the best in the world.

This discovery set me off on a new mission. I decided to embark on a thorough investigation of the Springbok production line, and to try to identify the weak links, if any. It became a fascinating journey which took me to parts of the country I'd never normally venture into and gave me a whole new perspective on where we all are, in this dynamic, ever-shifting society of ours.

1 The Mothers

If there was one member of the benighted 2011 Rugby World Cup squad who summed up the 'what if' factor, it was Bismarck du Plessis. If he had not been snapping at captain John Smit's heels, there might not have been the same level of vilification hurled at Smit. And if he, instead of Smit, had been in the starting line-up at the fateful quarterfinal against the Wallabies, might his explosiveness not have made a difference? After Heinrich Brüssow had left the field, might Bismarck have been the one player who could have countered David Pocock in the wild west of the breakdown?

Bismarck and Jannie du Plessis don't only play together at national level. They are also the enforcers of the Sharks team; the hooker and the tighthead prop, shoulder to shoulder at the muscle end of the game: the scrum.

Most media attention had been focused on Bismarck, for the tragedy of his being overlooked, for his very public fury and disappointment, for his evident talent. But Jannie seems to me equally interesting. He is the one Bok who manages to run a parallel career and, being the older of two very close siblings, provides another perspective on his more famous brother. To understand what made them, I travelled to Bethlehem, the auspiciously named town in the rural Free State where they were born and raised.

Jannie had given me his mother's cell number, but, as it turned out, I had some difficulty setting up an appointment to see her. Her phone was never answered and there was no voicemail facility. I thought perhaps she didn't want to talk to me, and was ready to respect that, but thought I would give it one last try in case it was simply a matter of mis-communication. I knew that she taught at Voortrekker High School in Bethlehem, so I took a chance and pitched up at the reception one chilly morning in the winter of 2012 and asked to speak to her.

A few minutes later, she walked into the school lobby, an imposing woman with Jannie's broad, open face. She said that she had a class and couldn't talk to me then but she would meet me in the coffee shop of the local Mica store when school finished at 14.30.

While I waited for her, I did some exploring. Bethlehem, despite its biblical name, is fairly unremarkable, a dusty transit town centred around the main road, through which a procession of trucks trundles its way to and from the N3 and, from there, either down to the port at Durban or north to the consumer hub of Gauteng.

On its southern edges, beauty looms in the form of the golden sandstone crags that mark the start of the Dra-kensberg. Just 10km south of Bethlehem is the Du Plessis farm, on the road to the fashionable hilltop village of Clarens, upon which thousands of tourists converge each weekend for a dose of art, haute cuisine and hiking in the surrounding mountains.

But there wasn't time to take a drive out there, and not much to do in Bethlehem itself, so I headed for the Mica store and settled down to wait for Jo-Helene. Mica is a large, warehouse-type store stocking everything from crockery to farming implements. In the adjacent coffee shop, farmers' wives meet their friends and fuel up on homemade cake before picking children up from school. From my morning's exploration, I know that this cheerful, unpretentious place is about as classy as Bethlehem gets.

Jo-Helene sweeps in, dead on 14.30, greeting people to her left and right as she makes her way to the table where I am sitting, in a quiet corner at the back of the coffee shop. There is a brief getting-to-know-each-other interlude. Jannie has told her it's okay to speak to me, otherwise she wouldn't have. She is protective of her sons' privacy. I apologise for my halting Afrikaans, but she is quite comfortable in English. In truth, I feel like a bit of a tourist. Rural white communities feel like alien territory. I am on the alert for hostile value systems such as racism and apartheid nostalgia. But I soon warm to Jo-Helene, and, after two hours, feel so much admiration for her that she's stayed in my mind ever since.

First, she explains the family's cultural heritage.

Bismarck is named after Jo-Helene's father. His own father was ardently pro-German, having experienced British barbarism in the form of the Anglo-Boer War concentration camps, and, as a result, Britain's enemy was his friend.

When his first son was born in 1915, during the First World War, he christened him Bismarck Wilhelm, after Otto von Bismarck, the 19th-century Prussian statesman who united the disparate states to create modern Germany. Bismarck Wilhelm Ficks settled in Clocolan in the Free State, and he and his wife produced three children, one of whom was Jo-Helene.

Bismarck Ficks, clearly a man ahead of his time, insisted his children learn to speak seSotho. It was not possible to live happily in South Africa unless you were intimate with at least one African language, he said. Jo-Helene Ficks went on to study it at the University of the Orange Free State, and, after graduating, she taught seSotho and Afrikaans at the local teachers' training college.

At 27, she married Francois du Plessis, who was nine years older, and they went to live on his family farm outside Bethlehem.

Jannie was born on 16 November 1982. Eighteen months later, on 22 May 1984, Jo-Helene gave birth to Bismarck. Both nature and nurture conspired to give the boys a sporting chance at excellence. Jo-Helene had run the 400m and played netball for her province while Francois had played prop, also for his province. The boys grew up going to rugby and netball matches.

Did she and Francois set out to make Springboks out of their sons, I ask.

Not particularly, she replies. She thinks it was more a matter of how they were brought up and the lifestyle they imbibed from their parents. Both Jo-Helene and her husband involved the boys in everything they did. The fact that they were 'older parents' helped. She was 28 when she gave birth to Jannie – an advanced age to embark on motherhood in the rural Free State – and her husband was 37.

'I think as you get older, you realise how wonderful it is to have children. You put more into them.'

'The children,' as she still calls these two hulking men, were made to help out from a very early age, both in the house and on the farm. 'Small as they were, they helped me to lay the table and to wash up. They learnt to operate the milking machine. From very small, they had to help me and my husband on the weekends. That became their job: to milk the cows. That was how they learnt their love of cows.'

Whenever a cow was slaughtered for beef, the children were given their own knives so that they could participate. She and Francois took the time to teach the boys how to do each task safely and effectively.

It was the same with sport. 'Jannie was a bit chubby, but, if I decided they have to run cross-country, he would do it. I would train him.'

Bismarck was always the more athletic of the two. Jannie had to work at it. But, along with the technical skills, she taught them that other crucial life skill: perseverance. 'If someone tells them, "I'm not happy with your performance," they will work on it.'

And, following her father's advice that it was imperative to be familiar with an African language, she and Francois both spoke to them in seSotho and each of their children was given a Sotho name. Their third son is still known as Tabbi, a derivative of his seSotho name, Thabakgolo. Jannie and Bismarck first spoke to each other in Sotho. It was only when they went to boarding school at the age of six that they really learnt Afrikaans.

'My children never knew apartheid,' says Jo-Helene firmly.

The family was struck by tragedy in 1993 when Francois was diagnosed with early-onset Parkinson's disease. Jannie was only 15. Bismarck was in Grade 7. Their two youngest children were not yet at school. When I met Jo-Helene, she had just had to absorb another blow. A few weeks earlier, Francois had had a bad fall. Soon afterwards, the couple watched on TV the Sharks playing one of the Super 15 games. Afterwards, she had turned to him and remarked what a fantastic spectacle it had been. His response was yes, it was a very good movie. 'I realised he had not recognised the children.' She phoned Jannie and they agreed Francois needed to undergo tests to confirm what they both suspected: his illness now included dementia.

I quickly understood that a few missed calls in a life as hectic as hers would easily have gone unnoticed. At that point, Jo-Helene was driving 10km into Bethlehem every day to teach English and seSotho at Voortrekker High School. She was also the school's netball coach. At night, when her husband's carer left for the day, she tended to all his needs. She oversaw the finances for the farm and for the two adjoining farms, now owned by Jannie and Bismarck. After many false starts, they currently have an excellent live-in manager, Wolker, who runs all three farms, so at least she has some help there.

Her youngest child, a girl, is a boarder at Voortrekker High, but she comes home at weekends, and it is Jo-Helene who has to stay up to fetch her when she goes to parties on a Saturday night.

I met Jo-Helene on a Thursday afternoon. Early the following morning, she was taking her netball team to Welkom for the Free State championships, which would last through the weekend. She had found someone to stay with Francois on the Friday night, but on Saturday, after the games were over, she would drive 180km back to the farm to spend the night with him and then return to Welkom on Sunday morning in time for the first match.

I marvel at this; it sounds utterly exhausting. She says:

'I decided years and years ago that, where the children and my husband are concerned, I will never get tired. Even if your husband is ill, you have to go on as if it's a normal household. Which it's not.' Like her sons, Jo-Helene feels bolstered by her strong Christian faith. 'I am guided by a higher hand,' she tells me.

Teaching for her is both a vocation and a passion. And I imagine she is a very good teacher. Bethlehem is a small place, and one peopled by her past pupils, including our waitress, a young black woman. *'Dankie, my kind,'* she says to the girl who places before her a steaming bowl of homemade butternut soup.

The childhood she gave her two sons was in some ways singular: the openness to another culture, one at the time largely despised by the rest of the white community. The emphasis on excellence. But, in many ways, it was also a typical rural Afrikaans childhood as Jannie, now embedded in a very English Durban, was to point out to me.

* * *

The significance of genes is also clear in the make-up of another great Springbok, Jean de Villiers. His father, Andre, was a Western Province lock. His mother, Louise, was in the provincial netball team. Jean also scored on the nurturing front. Louise, like Jo-Helene du Plessis, is a teacher and a netball coach. This professional expertise in the development and training of kids must have been of great help to their respective sons. And, like the Du Plessis family, the De Villiers family comes from a small, closely knit community.

But there are also big differences. The essence of Jannie and Bismarck is of highly evolved sons of the soil, of a solid power pack – resourceful, self-reliant, but with a twist of sophistication. In car terms, I'd put them down as Land Rovers or Toyota Land Cruisers: top of the range with every conceivable electronic aid.

Jean is more finely tuned, quick in both wit and pace. There is a sensitivity and emotional intelligence about him that lends itself to intuitive and highly effective leadership.

Jean grew up in the genteel Cape winelands town of Paarl, an hour's drive from Cape Town. His parents, who have lived there all their lives, are now renting a house on a golf estate on the edge of the town 'while Andre decides whether he wants to retire or not', says Louise. I am sitting with her on her veranda, overlooking a lake alive with wild geese and framed by manicured green grass. In the distance loom blue-hazed mountains. It's beautiful and tranquil, and the coffee she has made me is very good. Louise has just had an operation on her knee and is on crutches. She used the same surgeon who operated on Jean's knee and she spent hours in the gym prior to the op strengthening the ligaments and muscles around the knee in order to hasten her recovery. Louise thinks like an athlete. For the past eleven years, she has been selling property, but she is now 'a lady of leisure'. She appears anything but: despite the crutches, she comes across as a vigorous, spirited woman.

A few years back, she and Andre sold the house, on the slopes of the mountain, in which the boys grew up. While Jean was in Ireland, playing for Munster, they lived in his house in Bellville to care for his dogs. Since Jean's return with his wife, Marlie, they have been renting this house on the golf estate. Their real home is their beach house in De Kelders, to which they will retire. When Andre is ready.

At school, Louise played tennis and badminton and swam and played netball in the provincial teams. She went on to do a BA in Physical Education at Stellenbosch University and then got a teaching job at her alma mater, the dual-medium Paarl girls' school, La Rochelle. She had two sons: the first-born was Andre-Louis, whose arrival was followed a year later by Jean. 'Jean never slept. He was a colic baby,' she says with a sigh.

From birth, both boys were extremely active. By the time he was nine months old, Jean was swimming.

Were you planning to rear a Springbok, I ask her. Not at all, she says.

'We never pushed them in any direction. Even though my husband played rugby for Western Province, they were never encouraged to play rugby above hockey or tennis. Both of them were very good sportsmen. It's in the genes.

'We let them take part in as many activities as they wanted to and there was never any pressure to be the best. Only when they got to high school did they have to choose. The only thing I taught them was that, whatever you do, at sport or at school, you must do it to the best of your ability. Either you go flat out or you don't do it at all.

'I always tried to stimulate them: both intellectually and physically. I played cricket with them. I played rugby with them.'

When they started doing well at sport, Louise gave up her teaching job, although she continued to coach both swimming and the provincial netball team.

'My mother was very active in sport, so she never had time to spend next to the sports field when I was involved. So I decided that, when I had children, I would be there for them. I would be there to support them.'

Like Francois and Jo-Helene du Plessis, Louise and Andre brought their children up to be bilingual, although in the case of the De Villiers family, their second language was English. 'I used to sit with them when they were in the bath and teach them the English words for everything. You need English. I know it is very important in business and in sport.' I had noticed on the coffee table in the lounge a pile of books by Jo Nesbø, the edgy Norwegian thriller writer. Louise has been reading them during the inactivity enforced by her operation. She is as at ease in English as she is in Afrikaans. As is Jean.

Andre de Villiers owned the town's sports shop and also used to supply the local schools and prisons with uniforms. Like Louise, he was a very engaged parent. To this day, he travels to every game Jean plays in, wherever in the world it is. But, when the boys were growing up, he was frequently away on business and Louise was left in charge.

'My children lacked for nothing, but they were not spoilt. I raised them very strictly. Discipline was my responsibility. I raised them to have respect for each and every person, no matter who they were. If they were older, they called them 'oom' or 'tannie'.

'There were certain rules that were non-negotiable, such as, you don't lie. Face up to what you've done and take the consequences. I used to go berserk if they told me a lie.'

Like Bismarck and Jannie, the De Villiers brothers are very

close. 'They would travel to the ends of the earth for each other. Andre-Louis was always extremely protective towards Jean. He always took the brunt of whatever they did so Jean got away with murder at times.'

Not always, though.

Both she and, later, Jean, told me about an incident when Andre-Louis was in matric and Jean in Grade 11. 'My mom wasn't happy with our maths so she organised extra classes in maths and accounting. The guy who gave the classes was our first team coach. My brother had his licence so we would drive to the rugby field and sit there and he would read a book and I'd go and see my girlfriend. We would take the money and not go to the classes. After a couple of months, my mom saw that our marks weren't improving so she came to rugby practice and asked the coach after practice: if they are coming to the classes, why aren't their marks improving?'

Jean says, grinning: 'He gave her the news that we had never been to a class that year. When we got home, my mom welcomed us with a nice klap. To this day, we still laugh about that.'

2 The Schools

At the Truida Kestell primary school in Bethlehem, the headmaster introduces me to Anmar van Biljon, who was Jannie du Plessis's teacher in Grade 5, when he was 11 years old. Anmar glows at the mention of his name.

'Jannie always had a smile on his face. He was a lovable child and he had a very good sense of humour. He was a very nice kid to teach. When they went from one class to another, he was always reading. In class, when he finished work, he was reading. That is very unusual for a boy. And he was a leader. When he was in Grade 7, Jannie was on the student council. He was a prefect.'

His academics were excellent. 'He came near the top of the class.'

Bismarck was not nearly as satisfactory.

'He was the opposite of Jannie. He was already this strong *mannetjie* [little man] and he was quite mischievous. I think his mind was always on: what are we going to do next break? And the games were quite rough because they tackle and wrestle. Bismarck was very competitive. He always wanted to win.'

The family struggled financially. 'On the farm, the boys had to work. They had responsibilities. Children who grow up in a hostel get used to rules. They can't be spoilt.'

The brothers still visit. 'They are very loyal and very grounded,' she enthuses. 'It's wonderful when such important learners come back to visit you.' She always reminds Jannie, she says, that when he goes overseas, he must ask questions, look around him.

As I get up to leave, I comment: 'You must have far more black kids now?' She grimaces and looks away.

'Yes,' she says tightly. 'And I'm very glad Bismarck is not here now!'

'Why?'

'Because he would have played with them!'

Bully for Bismarck, I think. I look at the principal. Surely he would rebuke her? He turns his face away and says nothing.

So she encouraged the sunny, fair-haired Jannie to open his mind through reading and travel. But to his dark-skinned compatriots she would prefer it to remain closed.

It was break time as I left the school. A few black kids were playing together in the grounds, all neat and spruce in the Truida Kestell uniform. Like any other small child – like Jannie du Plessis – all they probably wanted to do was to please their teacher. I wondered if these tender, impression-able little souls had yet awakened to the fact that, no matter how hard they tried with this particular teacher, all they were ever likely to evoke was contempt.

Schools – particularly high schools – are the bedrock of South African rugby.

The 251 Springboks capped since 1992 come from 143 high schools. Forty per cent of them come from just 21 schools.

Jo-Helene says she wanted the boys to stay in Bethlehem for high school, progressing up the hill to the coeducational Voortrekker High School where she now teaches. But they insisted on going to Grey College in Bloemfontein because that was where their dad and their maternal grandfather had gone. 'I remember the first time we took Jannie there,' she muses. 'There was a photograph of my father on the wall and he said: *"Dis oupa Bismarck! Dis hoekom ek hier moet wees."'* ('That's grandpa Bismarck! That is why I must come here.')

Grey Bloem, as it is more commonly known, is also the incubator of more Springboks than any other school. Since 1992, when South African rugby officially became non-racial and was readmitted to the global game, Grey Bloem has produced 22 Springboks.

Grey is one of South Africa's oldest schools, with its roots in British colonial rule. The school's website records that 'The then Governor of the Cape Colony, Sir George Grey, visited the new Republic of the Orange Free State and on 13 October 1855 donated a sum of money towards the establishment of an institution for higher education. The school was officially opened on 17 January 1859, with dr. Andrew Murray as the first headmaster. The Model Republic, Bloemfontein and Grey College grew and developed together.' During the apartheid era, it would have been whites-only and a faithful purveyor of white-supremacist Christian National Education. It has shown an impressive capacity for reinvention. New buildings have been built on the original site; older buildings have been modernised. Classes are taught in both English and Afrikaans, and the school declares its ethos to be one of 'moderation and tolerance' and aspires to equip all its boys for a multicultural society.

Assembly is conducted in English one week and Afrikaans the next. The same practice is followed in the hostel. One of its old boys, Springbok hooker Tiaan Liebenberg, told me that one of his best friends at school was Taiwanese. There was easy mingling between the Afrikaans classes – mostly white, but with a few coloured kids – and the English classes, which were mostly South African black kids, but with a sprinkling of foreign kids, including Japanese and Tiaan's Taiwanese mate. Tiaan said that, since leaving school, he thought that this diversity had given him an edge over boys from, say, Pretoria's Afrikaanse Hoër Seunskool ('Affies'), which is uniformly Afrikaans, with some coloured kids, as it enabled him to deal more easily with the multicultural demands of a globalised game.

I arrive at Grey for a visit and find the staircase leading to the central building blocked by a straggle of black kids, who seem impervious to my polite requests to let me through. When I make it through to the entrance hall, that too is full of black kids, and some beautiful singing emerges from the open doors of the school hall, another flight up. At the reception desk, I ask for Johan Volsteedt, the director of rugby, with whom I have an appointment. He leads me through to a small office, where he explains that every Friday they have assembly and a concert with a neighbouring school for disabled kids, who are mainly deaf and dumb and mainly black. So that's it, then. They couldn't hear me.

'It helps our boys to see others are not as fortunate as they are,' he explains. I'd been expecting a militaristic, testosterone-driven establishment, so all this – the nonchalant black kids and the understated altruism – is a pleasant surprise. I'd noticed on the Grey website that the school had recently had a visit from Angus Buchan, the Christian evangelist who espouses conservative family values, with the man as head of the household and the woman in the kitchen. I remark on this to Johan. Some of the parents organised it, he says. It wasn't the school.

Grey alumni are immensely generous to their alma mater and this helps the school to provide superlative sports facilities in every code. In winter, rugby has to compete with soccer and hockey. Around 350 of their boys play rugby, says Johan, and only 40 of those are black.

For those who choose rugby, the demands and the competition are intense. 'We have practice every afternoon, and they come to the gym in the morning and we tour a lot. Even if you make it into the first team, you are always under pressure. The player knows that, if he is not pulling his weight, there is someone waiting for his position.'

Johan coached both Bismarck and Jannie du Plessis in their last two years of school rugby. It's hard to imagine it now but Bismarck didn't make the first team when he was in Grade 11. Nor was he first choice for Craven Week. But he struck lucky. 'Bismarck played for our second team – which we call the Cherries. But then the first-team hooker was injured before going to Craven Week and Bismarck came in as replacement. And at the same time he got into the SA Schools team.

'He was 17. In his matric year, he played first team as well.

'Jannie was a very motivated player and he worked very hard. Bismarck was quieter and never talked much, but he was a strong, physical player and you could see already that both of them, particularly Bismarck, were destined for bigger things.'

Jannie also played first-team, so the brothers played together, hooker and tighthead prop, arms around each other's necks, as they are today. Bismarck is the more vulnerable, though, because both his arms are pinned behind him. He trusts his brother to prop him up.

It isn't a surprise that they have done so well, he says: 'Because they had both the talent and the drive. And academically, they were both good, too.'

Jannie and Bismarck have come back to the school to speak at assembly. 'We are very proud of our old boys,' says Johan.

And they continue to do the school proud. In Heyneke Meyer's 2012 Rugby Championship squad, there were ten Grey College old boys: Jannie and Bismarck, Adriaan Strauss, Francois Steyn, Tiaan Liebenberg, Flip van der Merwe, CJ van der Linde, Johan Goosen, Ruan Pienaar and Coenie Oosthuizen. In the game against Argentina at Newlands on 18 August, all three hookers in the squad – Bismarck, Adriaan Strauss and Tiaan Liebenberg – were Grey old boys.

✶ ✶ ✶

The school that has produced the second-highest number of Springboks since 1992 is Paarl Gimnasium. Its tally is ten, well below that of Grey College but four higher than that of its closest competitors. It is another venerable school, established in 1858, around the same time as Grey College, for the purpose of fostering the Afrikaans language and providing a Christian education. Above the school, on Paarl mountain, looms the monument to the Afrikaans language. Yet Paarl Gim wears this history lightly. Chatting with the acting principal, Jeanette Gersbach, in her large, airy office, I get a sense of a modern institution. For a start, it is coed, with an easy racial mix. I ask Jeanette what proportion of the pupils are of colour and she shrugs: 'We don't count,' she says. 'To us, they are just children.'

All tuition is in Afrikaans, though, which will automatically limit the numbers of black pupils. And it is consciously Christian. But a non-Christian child or an atheist would not be excluded, she says firmly.

I'd always heard of the school in relation to rugby, so I had assumed it was an all-boys institution. It started off that way. It was only in the 1960s that girls were admitted. Now there are around 500 of each gender. Organised sports have been offered since 1901, and competitions were at club level before the advent of interschool derbies.

The elegant buildings in the centre of Paarl, initially occupied by the entire school, now house only the primary school. In the 1960s, two farms on the slopes of the mountain were bought and the present, equally imposing, buildings erected for a separate senior school, surrounded by 13ha of grounds.

It is an extremely well-resourced school, with swimming pool, rugby and cricket fields, tennis courts and an Astro-Turf field for hockey, all within the school grounds. Athletics and cross-country running are also offered. Girls play netball, and boys cricket and rugby. Otherwise, all sports are open to both genders. Jeanette says it is through sport that it is easiest to integrate. 'The parents support the teams together. It makes it much easier for families from different races to mix.'

Competition for admission is intense. The criteria include academic achievements and interest in sport and culture. 'We need students who are involved in school life so they must participate in at least one sport in summer and one in winter. If they don't play, they must be involved in some way because we believe that, if they are busy and involved, they are happier and it prepares them better for life after school.

'We look at their values: if they were brought up well. We look for respect, for kids who take part in the community, who can fit in.

'What we want is to foster kids who will be different and can accept difference in others. We want them to leave here prepared for life. That is one of the reasons we have both boys and girls.'

Tuition costs R15 300 a year – not bad for the quality of education provided. Boarding costs an extra R23 000. Almost half the kids are boarders; they come from nearby farms and further upcountry. There are even a couple from Gauteng. Friendships are made here which last for life. 'The kids are very happy here,' she says. 'I think sometimes they enjoy school too much!'

As with Grey Bloem, alumni are well organised and generous. It is not unusual to find second and third generations of families being educated here. Annual reunions are timed to coincide with the interschool rugby derby with Paarl Boys' High and they bring the town to a standstill. Paarl Boys' High also organises its reunions for that time of year, and crowds of 20 000 are common. In 2012, six different Paarl Gim year groups, ranging from the 2007 matric year to 1992 matrics, celebrated reunions during the derby.

Although rugby is the most glamorous sport, the school 'works very hard not to make, say, the hockey players, feel inferior. We try to give them the same opportunities.

'We use rugby to obtain sponsorship for other sporting codes, so we know how important rugby is for the school. Rugby games are televised so it is important that the name of the school is highlighted. We have had the same jersey since the beginning, so it is well known. We use the publicity rugby gets to enhance the Gim brand.'

The school's annual matric pass rate is 96%. There are 55 teachers, only 32 of whom are paid by the state. The rest are paid for out of funds raised by the school.

Springbok kicking coach Louis Koen is a Paarl Gim old boy, as is referee Marius Joubert and Bok players Schalk Burger and Ashley Johnson. And, of course, Jean de Villiers.

Jeanette Gersbach taught Jean accounting in grades 10, 11 and 12. He matriculated in 1999. 'He was the first schoolboy that I can remember who had a handwriting concession for the matric exam – that tells the examiner that this candidate has a problem with handwriting.'

But she adored him, she says. 'The other kids used to say he was my *witbroodjie* [favourite] and maybe he was.

'He was not the best student I've ever had because he was not that interested in schoolwork. But he did quite well with little effort.

'He was very popular among the kids as well as the teachers. He was the vice head boy of the school in matric and he was vice captain of the rugby team.

'He liked playing tricks on this fellow students.'

I ask Jeanette what she thought were the crucial components in the making of a Springbok. Coaches are the most important, she says. 'After that, teachers. But it must also be something to do with the way they are brought up. The way they encourage themselves and the way in which they believe in themselves.'

It's also necessary for the school to manage them properly. Individuals must not become bigger than the school. 'We want them to be part of the school community, part of the town. We don't want them to carry on all on their own. They must play their part in the school and they must know where they fit in.'

She recalls the fuss around Handré Pollard in 2011 – while he was in matric, both Western Province and the Blue Bulls were fighting over him, and in the end he went with the latter. 'He got so much publicity that it could have impacted negatively on his school and sport career. But we gave him the certainty that, when he came back after the Under-20 World Cup [IRB Junior World Rugby Trophy], he was treated as a normal school kid. I think he felt safe in that.'

I ask her about Schalk, and she reveals she was his mentor in Grade 9. 'He was a challenging kid in school. He liked to challenge the rules.' Like Jean, he was a very talented sportsman. 'I remember at one stage, he had to decide whether to carry on with cricket or rugby.'

And what makes a good school, I ask? What advice would she have for a failing school? She thinks for a minute and then says: 'Everyone must be working towards a specific vision and it must be generally accepted that the most important thing is the students. So, in everything you do in a school, the interest of the kids must be at the forefront. You must put the kids' interests first. If you lose that focus, you have a problem.'

She believes teachers should be involved in sport because

they know the educational value of sport. 'So, if we have a coach from outside the school community, we give them a teacher to act as manager of the team in order to keep the educational aspects going.'

This is still the kind of community where teachers are not expected to be paid extra for coaching, although things are changing. 'We have started paying them a little extra to teach sports. The younger generation want more money.'

Jeanette has known Jean de Villiers's parents most of her life. Both she and Louise de Villiers taught Myra Burger, Schalk junior's mother. What is also clear from looking at the Du Plessis brothers' and Jean de Villiers's backgrounds is that both families have built up deep reserves of social capital. There would have been a strong and secure community watching all three boys from their first steps, wishing the best for them and contributing their own accumulated skills and wisdom to their nurturing. I wondered also if Grey Bloem and Paarl Gim pupils benefit from the more complex social structures with which they grow up: bilingualism in the case of Grey Bloem and coeducation in the case of Paarl Gim. In both cases, pupils will from an early age easily incorporate difference in others: for Grey Bloem, a different language and culture; for Paarl Gim, another gender.

3 The Bok Brothers

The route to professionalism starts early. Boys with potential are picked out at an early age by scouts from the major unions – at Craven Weeks or as a result of tip-offs from rugby coaches at leading schools. They are signed up with paying contracts either before they leave school or immediately afterwards.

Jannie and Bismarck du Plessis followed a different route.

Jannie enrolled at the University of the Free State (UFS) medical school. Bismarck registered at the same university a year later for a bachelor's degree in Commerce, specialising in Agricultural Economics. Jannie, in particular, is clearly an exceptional case in that, since he left school, he has contrived to run two extremely demanding careers at the same time. This ability to multi-task was first put to the test while he was a student, so, in 2012, I tracked down one of his UFS lecturers.

Professor Gert van Zyl is now Dean of the Faculty of Health Sciences and a very busy man, and it takes weeks and many phone calls to set up an appointment, but, once I'm there, it's worth it because he remembers Jannie well. He is a precise man, thin and dark-haired. We sit at the round conference table in his spacious office. He is anxious to impress upon me that it was not Jannie's rugby prowess that got him his highly sought-after place in medical school. 'He was selected for his academic achievements, not his sporting ones,' he says firmly. 'In the selection process, we do give credits for excelling in sport. But you can earn 120 points to be selected, and out of that 120, you can be given a maximum of four for sport. Jannie would have got three or four for his rugby.'

Nor did he automatically get leeway from the faculty. 'In his pre-clinical years, there wasn't such a challenge in accommodating him because his rugby commitments would take place after hours. But, when it came to his clinical rotation, there was a challenge.'

What made it feasible, he says, was that Jannie himself approached the problem with maturity and foresight. 'He communicated very well with senior academics within the faculty and that was what made the difference. For instance, a student can't come and tell me on Thursday that on Friday he is going away for a game. Each and every time, Jannie thought these things through and came and sat with us to work it out. He took that extra bit of ownership.'

He knew that he had additional responsibilities and he made a conscious decision to make it all work.

'We negotiated with Jannie that we were not going to give him time off, so, in the majority of cases, he worked out with module leaders how to put the time in.

'There was a commitment from the faculty side to make it achievable. There was from Jannie's side a passion to study medicine so that is why we went the extra mile to sort out his studies. We recognised that he had the passion and the discipline. No favours were done for him.

'We have had other sports people since then who studied medicine and we continuously go back to Jannie as an example – to say that, if you communicate and you plan in advance, you can make it work.'

Surely it is rare, I say, to see this kind of organisational skill in a student?

'It must be his family,' replies Van Zyl. 'Jannie's head was sorted out when he got here. We see brilliant students, and if they are not sorted out in their heads study-wise, we see them failing and dropping out.'

With some students – mainly black but also white – the dearth of family social capital takes its toll. 'You see a difference between first-generation students at higher education and those whose parents and grandparents had university education.' The university has a support unit for struggling students, and Jonathan Jansen, the current rector, takes it upon himself to make it as easy as possible for students from difficult backgrounds to succeed, but, for some, 'it remains a huge mountain to climb'.

Both Jannie and Bismarck were fortunate in that their mother not only had a degree from the same university but she had also worked as a lecturer at the teachers' training college. She knew what it took.

Gert van Zyl said Jannie's personality was a contributing factor. He easily made friends with classmates. 'So he was surrounded by a support group.'

In fact, I'd heard a story, partly from Jo-Helene and partly from Jannie, about a particular classmate who made a big difference, going to the length of signing Jannie into classes in his absence, and then lending him his notes so that he could catch up. Dennis was his name, and he and Jannie were both in Reitz hostel, although several years before it became notorious for the racist abuse of cleaners. But, even then, the hostel committee were a bullying bunch and tried to force Dennis to cut his long hair. Even though Jannie was only first-year, he stood up to the bullies and told them that, if they touched Dennis again, they'd have to deal with him first. And, first-year or not, he was, after all, a Grey Bloem prop. This sealed a friendship that was to give Jannie a lot of help in working the system.

It is particularly gratifying to Professor Van Zyl that Jannie is now practising as a doctor, partly because so much was invested in his education and training. Currently, students pay R25 000 a year, which is only 10% of the full cost. The taxpayer funds the rest.

In his last three years, Jannie did rotations in a psychiatric hospital, as well as in local state hospitals, Pelonomi and Universitas private hospitals, and various clinics. He ended up getting his degree in the minimum amount of time. 'And he wasn't just a 50% student. He did well.'

Professor Van Zyl says Jannie is now used as an example to students: 'We have sent some of them to speak to him. For us, it wasn't just doing it for Jannie – it's a culture in the faculty. We try to go the extra mile for students, especially if you get the feeling from students that they are passionate and committed and are not just trying to get extra favours.'

* * *

It was fortuitous that Bloemfontein rugby was going through something of a renaissance during the period that Jannie and Bismarck were students there. This was where they first encountered Jacques Nienaber, who was also in New Zealand for the 2011 Rugby World Cup, as defence coach for the Springboks. Jacques is now coaching with the Stormers and I arranged to meet him at the Western Province High Performance Centre in Bellville. I discover that Jacques's career in coaching was sparked by a friendship he formed while he was doing his military service.

He happened to be assigned to the Armoured Corps, together with Rassie Erasmus, now director of rugby at the South African Rugby Union (SARU). This all happened on the cusp of the transition to the democratic era, when military service ceased to be compulsory for white men. However, those who volunteered to stay on were well paid, and this is what Rassie did, rising to the rank of lieutenant. Nienaber enrolled for a degree in Physiotherapy at the UFS. Later, Rassie signed up for a Movement Science degree and played for the UFS rugby team, the Shimlas. In 2005, Rassie started coaching the provincial team, the Cheetahs, and he asked Jacques to be conditioning coach. It turned out to be a stellar year for the team. For the first time in 25 years, they won the Currie Cup.

Jacques had known Jannie since he was in the under-21s. 'He is one of the hardest workers I have ever encountered. It is a massive challenge to both study and play rugby. In professional rugby, you seldom see it. But it personifies Jannie. After we won the Currie Cup, we all went out celebrating, but he went straight back to his books because his exams started that Monday.'

At the same time, he managed to keep himself in good condition and to avoid injury. 'He was one of my fittest props. He can run with the locks and loosies. Jannie always wanted to work a bit harder. He would say: "Jacques, I want to improve my agility." I said: "Skip." The next day, he bought a skipping rope.'

He did get injured once. 'We did an assessment on the guys' passing skills and we laughed at Jannie: he passed that ball into the ground. We said "Jannie, don't worry about it. You're a prop, you don't have to pass the ball!" The next day, he was in the gym.

'He came to me and said: "There is something wrong; I can't lift weights on one side." We sent him for an MRI scan and he had a lesion in the C6 neck disc. It had a bulge pushing on the nerve. On the inside, a disc is like chewing gum so it can protrude and bulge through. The protrusion then irritates the nerve.' When the whole thing bulges through and lies against the nerve, it requires surgery to clean it out. This is the operation Schalk Burger had in 2006. The consequence for Jannie was strength and sensory loss. He had no feeling in his thumb and his biceps lacked strength.

'So that was what we picked up in the passing exercise: there was no power in the pass. Some orthopods would have said we had to operate and fuse the discs. But we went the conservative route. He worked on stabilising his deep neck flexors and his biceps to get the strength back.

'It is irritating work. "Stabilise" is a swear word in rugby: it's small, contracting movements. It's like Pilates; you've got to concentrate and control. Rugby players like big movements.

'The easy option would have been the op, but, for me, that's Jannie.' He won't take the short cut. 'Jannie will always say: "What can I do off the field to improve?" He is a hard worker. To be a doctor and play professional rugby is tough.'

The Cheetahs were a family under Rassie, says Jacques.

'Jannie was a massive Rassie man. We hadn't won the Currie Cup in 25 years so we were building towards that. Rassie came up with the plan that we would have three props on the bench, which was unheard of. Rassie felt we had to rotate our props to be dominant.'

Jannie was not the first choice prop. CJ van der Linde was. So Jannie was not initially paid to play.

But it was an exhilarating time for Free State rugby. The Cheetahs took home the Currie Cup again in 2006 and 2007.

Jacques didn't know Bismarck as well because the latter left UFS in 2004. He was captain of the Under-21s and the Sharks offered him a contract. He moved to Durban, completing his degree by correspondence. Jannie stayed until he graduated from medical school in 2007.

'Jannie and Bismarck know what they want. When they started earning money, they said: "We won't buy cars and houses. We are farmers." They took that money and bought cows. They always knew they wanted to farm. They had to grow up quickly. Jannie knew he couldn't stuff around first year because he studied with a loan. He and Bismarck are also probably the most competitive people I have met. Failure is not part of their make-up. It was not an option. Some players who come from rich families are different: they see it as fun.'

Others are catapulted into a fantasy world. 'A player gets his car sponsored and his boots sponsored and a million rand at the age of twenty and he thinks this is the real world. It's not!'

Jannie and Rassie hit it off because they shared this intense competitiveness: 'Rassie said in that first year: "We are the underdog but we can't think making a semi is good enough. We have to think differently. Jannie is all about that. He was never the best but he was prepared to work." '

Even though he wasn't first choice prop at the Cheetahs it never occurred to him to try elsewhere. 'Most guys would go to a different union to bypass if there was an incumbent in their position. Jannie said no, I will learn from this guy and wait my turn.'

'That is Jannie: he gets there through hard work. The oke who isn't so talented has to work hard. But hard work will always beat talent if talent doesn't work hard enough. Jannie was never the talented guy – he had to work harder than the next guy to get there.

'CJ van der Linde, for instance, is an amazing physical specimen. He is an unbelievably explosive, huge specimen. Jannie is not that big; when he started playing tighthead at Free State, he was 106kg, which is same weight as loose forwards. A tighthead should be 116 to 124. Jannie was playing Currie Cup at 108kg. So his technique had to compensate for his weight. Now he is 122, now he's big. But he's big from gym. It wasn't a God-given weight. He had to work to get there.'

* * *

One lovely summer's evening in 2012, I set out for La Lucia, the upmarket Durban suburb where Jannie and Bismarck live. I pull up at the top of the steep drive and Jannie comes out to greet me, dressed in shorts and a T-shirt. His feet are bare. The house is a Tuscan-style double-storey on the crest of a hill with sweeping lawns and a clear view of the Indian Ocean.

It looks as close to a farmyard as a front garden in a posh suburb can get. Two large dogs frolic around him. A couple of Egyptian geese, accompanied by a flotilla of youngsters, have occupied the swimming pool. Cute, I say. 'Not so cute when they start squawking at five o'clock in the morning. Bismarck just opens his window and shouts: "Fok off!" That usually works,' grins Jannie. He has already had a full day: practice at Kings Park at 7am; then all morning at the hospital; then back to Kings Park for the afternoon training session.

The house is full of people. Some family friends are occupying the main lounge. Bismarck and a friend are chatting in what looks like a family room. Jannie and I go into the kitchen, where he makes coffee for everyone, including the family friends, whom he calls 'tannie' and 'oom'. It's strange for me to see this 30-year-old man – a doctor, nogal – addressing in this way people who don't look much more than about ten years older than him. And addressing them in the respectful third person.

The room is spotlessly clean and tidy. This was shortly before Jannie's marriage to Ronel, and the brothers were living here alone. I am struck by Jannie's meticulousness. He brings two mugs of coffee to the long, polished dining room table where I am sitting, and then goes back to the kitchen for a china teaspoon holder on which to put the spoons. He has already sugared the coffees.

Wanting to get it out of the way because I know how painful the subject still is, I start off by asking him about the World Cup.

He starts slowly: 'Firstly there was the sendoff at Nelson Mandela Square. It's my fondest memory ever. It was surreal to be there. Rugby is a sort of war with rules and you are chosen to represent your country in something that only comes around every four years. And then the campaign ends in defeat! I think most guys ask themselves: could I have contributed in a different way to make it successful?

'I can't recall that anybody lacked commitment, and that brings peace, because it is something you can't control. Even if you never smoke a cigarette, you can't be assured of not getting lung cancer, so there we were doing everything in our power to get a good outcome and it didn't go that way. I don't know how we could have done it any better. We did everything right. We travelled properly; we ate right. We trained piss-hard.

'But we didn't make it. Now, three months later, it still hurts. It hurts a lot. But, if you think of what you put in, it brings a little comfort.'

Like the rest of the team, he is effusive in his praise for Peter de Villiers. 'We had a wonderful, person-orientated coach. He copped a lot of flak from people who didn't understand him, but anyone who spent any time with him knew he had a beautiful heart. There was no evil in him.

'People didn't understand him. Coach spoke to me more on one tour than any previous Bok coach spoke to me in four years. He cared for the players because he needed them to perform because he was out on the axe.'

And, as with the other players, he won't criticise any of his team members. But, of course, he believes that no one is better in his position than his brother.

Both brothers were delighted when Rassie Erasmus and Jacques Nienaber joined the Bok coaching team as technical and defence advisers because they had started their professional careers with them in Bloemfontein.

'It was catching up because he was our coach at the Cheetahs and Jacques Nienaber was our fitness coach and did our defence at Free State. It was wonderful to talk to him about the game and how he sees it. These are guys we went through wars with, and sometimes we lost really badly and sometimes we won.'

So why did they lose that particular quarterfinal? Jannie believes referee Bryce Lawrence was a factor.

'Rugby is unfortunately a game where a referee can play a big part. At ruck time, you either penalise the guy for holding onto the ball or for not releasing, so the line between right and wrong is very thin, although we can't blame Bryce entirely because we had opportunities to score and we missed them. Fourie was over the tryline twice and he lost the ball. Pat Lambie scored a try from a forward pass. We had opportunities to beat them, so to blame Bryce would be wrong, but to say his interpretation of the law had a big impact on the game is a fact.

'The way he refereed the breakdown made the impact of a player like David Pocock much bigger. Unfortunately Heinrich Brüssow got injured and we didn't have a guy who could compete with Pocock head to head.'

Should we have committed more guys to the breakdown?

'We had more than 72% of the ball in the whole game so I don't think it's to do with us sending too few people into the breakdown. If we do keep the ball, that means we are sending the right number of people to the breakdown, because there was an emphasis on attacking rugby from the beginning of

2010, when they said that they wanted benefit to go to the team carrying the ball, rather than the defending team, to make rugby more viewer-friendly. If you go on that, then the team that carries the ball for 72% of the game should be able to win the game, and we didn't. So, again, I don't think we used our chances as well as we could have and I don't think Bryce did us any favours, but you have to wonder whether there was a bigger hand in all of this.

'I firmly believe that we would have beaten the All Blacks. I felt that our team was pretty good, and we were playing constructive rugby, so I believe we would have beaten them. If you look at what they went through with Christchurch, and what a big thing the World Cup was for the whole population of 4.5 million people, then, in the greater scheme of the things, wasn't it the right thing to happen? I mean, you've got to ask yourself these questions.

'If you look at 1995, the All Blacks had a more exciting, more experienced team than ours, but ours won on guts, and, whether Nelson Mandela was the difference or that they played at home, that win meant a lot in a very important time for our country. You've got to ask: isn't it the same for New Zealand?'

He gets up and opens a drawer in the elegant cabinet edging the wall. His movements are economical and decisive: this is clearly a man who knows where everything in his kitchen and dining room is. But the move hides his face from me briefly, and I wonder whether this is to conceal the emotion that so clearly wells up in him. He takes out a brown place mat and puts it down in front of me. He'd noticed I was still holding my mug, scared of scarring this beautiful table.

Sitting down again, he sighs. 'I reflect on this over and over and over. Sometimes when Bismarck and I are here at night, we replay the World Cup again and again.

'But, I mean,' he says, in a lighter tone, determinedly wrenching himself out of this dark obsessing. 'Here we are, in Durban, with its wonderful weather. The sun is shining. It's not life and death! I got back to work after the World Cup and a little boy came in. He's eleven and he has leukaemia! And I think: he's got leukaemia and I'm disappointed because I lost a rugby game.'

This bright brave face doesn't last long. The sombre tone is soon back. 'Actually, it does feel like someone in the family died. It does feel like you lost a loved one. You put all your energy and all your effort into a campaign and it doesn't succeed. It still hurts and will probably hurt forever. In fifty years' time, Bismarck and I will probably still be talking about that game. But the reality is that New Zealand won the World Cup 8-7 at home and that was wonderful for them.'

Why he is so confident we could have beaten the All Blacks?

'Traditionally, South African rugby is more structured around the set piece, so that is why the forward pack becomes more important. Because you need first-phase ball, you need your good scrum ball and you need your good line-out ball. And then you plan your attacks from there.

'Whereas New Zealand traditionally have more exciting individuals. They've got a guy like Jonah Lomu, who can score a try from nowhere. It's like these two ways of playing it: where one side is much more structured and much more planning goes into it and the other team plays on natural ability. While both have been successful in the past, I don't think there is a right way or a wrong way. I just think this is the way South African players play the game.

'In the past,' he adds hastily. 'It's not to say it will stay like this. If you look at past teams, when we were successful, we played a structured game. New Zealand also play a structured game, but they have more individuals who do stuff out of the box. You have different views. People say playing structured rugby benefits you in pressure situations because you know that, if this goes wrong, you just go back to what you've trained.

'Whereas if you play on natural ability and something goes wrong, and when the pressure is on, and you have little time to make a decision, then things might not go so well.'

So, under the intense pressure of a World Cup semifinal, our nerve would have held better than that of an injury-ridden All Blacks side counting too much on flair.

It must have helped the brothers to deal with the disappointment, having gone through the wars together. Like Bismarck, Jannie had wanted to become a farmer, 'but my mom said farming was too hard. When I got accepted into medicine at Bloem, I didn't know if I wanted to do it but then my dad said he had prayed about it and thought that the fact I'd been accepted meant I should do it. So I did. I thought maybe I could help my dad.

'I played rugby to pay for my studies. I never put my heart and soul into rugby. I didn't put all my eggs in one basket. My mom always said: "You've got to get a proper job." We could do whatever our hearts desired but we had to study and we had to finish our degrees.

'I was studying on a loan and getting deeper and deeper

into debt and I thought: shit, shouldn't I stop studying and start playing rugby rather? I did go through a difficult time when I thought: is this really what I want to do? But now I'm grateful to my mom because she was firm and insisted both Bismarck and I carry on studying.

'I'm a Christian and I believe in the Bible. I believe God made things work out for me supernaturally. For example, we had to write a test the same day I was playing the semifinal in the Vodacom Cup in 2004. I asked the professor in charge if I could write the test earlier. He said no – you can understand why. He thought I might leak it or something. But I was in despair about it. Because, ever since I had started doing both, everybody said to me you can't serve two gods. You can't study medicine and play rugby. So then I thought, is this the time when I've got to decide between rugby and studying? I prayed about it. I prayed fervently, I must say. Then, next thing, an SMS comes through on my phone. It says, *"Hello Jannie, dis Dr Cilliers, ek het gedink oor jou saak. Ek sal 'n ander toets vir jou stel. Jy kan Donderdag kom skryf."* ("Hello, Jannie, it's Dr Cilliers. I have thought about your case. I will set another test for you. You can come on Thursday to write it.") So he set up a test just for me!'

It feels quite odd: the juxtaposition between this powerful man and the sense of vulnerability inherent in his wholesale submission to an invisible force. It obviously gives him strength and helps him cope with his ferocious workload. It also makes him even more likeable, because there is no arrogance in the man. He does not take the credit for his achievements. He is all gratitude and humility.

He goes on: 'Things like that built my faith and made me

believe God wanted me to do rugby and medicine because otherwise He wouldn't have let it work out like that. I went down on my knees and thought: the Lord came through for me then. It will always be all right. That one incident impacted greatly on my life. So I finished my degree – I did my internship in Bloem. Then I applied to do my community service in Durban and started playing rugby for the Sharks.'

Bismarck had already been there for a couple of years, and Jannie moved in with him. 'It's really awesome,' says Jannie, 'having your best friend and blood brother living with you, sharing your experiences.'

I ask: don't you fight?

'We fight like cat and dog sometimes!' he exclaims. 'But we're old or big enough to get over it. We know we've got to get over it or otherwise we won't make it. We do get angry with each other but we just sort it out.'

His day job is at the Bluff Military Hospital. It caters for members of the army, former members and their dependants. He oversees the HIV clinic.

I ask about the contradiction: 'In your one life you are a healer and in the other, you donder [hit] people?' He answers with a laugh: 'Actually, it would be quite nice if you could donder people sometimes!'

The beauty of rugby for him, he says, is that you get to measure yourself physically against somebody. 'I watch these boxers; they've got to be fit; they've got to be fast; they've got to have sharp reflexes; they've got to be able to box for 15 rounds. They've got to be not scared to get hit. They've got to keep on advancing even when they know the hit is coming.

'It's a bit like rugby: you can't be scared of getting hit. The other guy has also trained hard to beat you physically. That is what happened in the World Cup: they wanted to win too.

'As a healer, I'd rather say I work with people to solve their problems.' So he's the modern doctor, then. Not the doctor-as-God of old, rather doctor-as-partner.

'Sometimes it involves healing, or it involves advice. It's an interesting job. Sometimes, in winter, I think that if I see another case of flu, my brain will burst. And then you get another case that interests you: you think, *jis*, I've never seen this before. And you read up on it and you think about it and you try out medication and say, this isn't working. And I phone my prof in Bloem and he says do this and this and then they come back and say they feel much better. You get a sense of satisfaction that is deeper than just money. You feel like you made a difference.'

Being immersed in HIV/Aids also means he is brought face to face with poverty. 'It makes you realise how fortunate you are to have a house, to have good food to eat, to have a mother who pushed you to study.'

Living in Durban also means that he and Bismarck are exposed to a different culture, one that is dominant and that they have to adjust to. Durban, he points out, is very English. (And Zulu, of course.) It's made him think a lot about the difference between the Afrikaners and the English.

'The English get brought up to be a little bit more open-minded, which can be a good and a bad thing. Afrikaans people are more strict. This is right. This is wrong. Black and white. That can also be good and bad. You need the broader, open-mindedness of the typical English guy, but you also need the discipline and right and wrong of the typical Afrikaans background.

'There is a big difference. Afrikaans people are brought up differently from English; we get the shit beaten out of us when we are naughty, whereas their parents will rather talk to them. We have to go to church on a Sunday. English kids can go to church: nobody's going to force them, but they go by choice. There's no right or wrong. It's just different. We are brought up to call people "oom" because you have to respect the older guy and we don't want to be familiar. You are brought up to believe you've got to respect the older guy. He knows more than you. Whereas the English don't call anybody "uncle" or "sir". They call them by their name.

'In the Boks, there are big cultural differences. I grew up on a farm and had a typical Afrikaans background. But it is good to see how others view life and think about it. Listen to the black guys and the coloured guys. Give your view and then give him his chance to state his view and then go and think about it: you don't have to agree, but you have to listen to how you see stuff and how he sees stuff.'

Before I leave, he takes me into his bedroom. He wants to show me that he is a reader. And, indeed, there are two floor-to-ceiling bookcases filled with books. Aside from the medical textbooks, there are *Atlas Shrugged* by Ayn Rand and various autobiographies of successful men, including Alan Sugar. And Victor Matfield – his mom gave that to him for Christmas. The next day, I drop off a copy of *Touch, Pause, Engage!* for him. The next time I see Jannie, I am impressed to find that he has read it cover to cover. He is indeed a reading man.

* * *

The year 2012 turns out to be an eventful one for the Du Plessis brothers. Bismarck is awarded an honours degree in Economics from Unisa. It's a remarkable achievement, given the ongoing intensity of his rugby career. Then Jannie gets married to a fellow doctor, Ronel, in a charming outdoor wedding near Clarens. In June, both brothers, as expected, are called up to Heyneke Meyer's Springbok squad and suddenly find themselves among a tiny senior group. The Springboks get caught up in stalled negotiations with SARU and end up playing for several months without contracts, which means they don't get paid. Which, for the prudent Du Plessis brothers, means that Bismarck does not go to the extra expense of finding alternative accommodation to give the newlyweds their space.

At one point during the World Cup in New Zealand, I had found myself walking down a hotel corridor behind Bismarck. He was barefoot, in shorts and a tight Springbok shirt. Muscles curved and bulged everywhere: legs, buttocks, back. He walked very straight and tall – an extraordinary physical specimen. He is 1.89m tall and weighs 115kg. He felt to me – all of 57kg, 1.62m and minimal muscle – like an altogether different branch of the species.

I caught up with him again in Cape Town in August 2012, just before the Springboks took on Argentina's Pumas in the first match of the Rugby Championship, the four-nation successor to the Tri Nations. This would be his fourth game under Heyneke Meyer. Finally, he is free of John Smit and is the Boks' first-choice hooker. How is it going? I ask. How is the new regime?

'I love Heyneke!' he exclaims. 'He sets a great example.

41

Everyone looks up to him. He is a really good man and passionate about his job.'

Sitting beside him on the patio of Cape Town's Cullinan Hotel, I am again struck by the intense physicality of the man, but, at the same time, I have a vision of the boisterous, gutsy little boy conjured up by his teacher. I ask: 'How was school for you?'

'Well,' he says, 'I was a boarder from sub A to matric and it was hard.

'From a really young age, I had to stand up for myself and I had to adapt to a new environment. It's tough and you miss your mom. It made me appreciate home more and made me appreciate my mom. From six years old, I was working from a schedule, whereas at home you do whatever you want. And being a boarder you have to share everything – your personal space, your sweets, your biltong. And you have to stand up for yourself.

'I spoke Sotho before I spoke Afrikaans and I went to boarding school to learn to speak Afrikaans. And I'm really blessed because I believe that, if we as South Africans want to go forward, we have to learn an African language. It shows respect and you learn a lot more about their culture and what's important to them. Speaking Sotho makes me good friends with Lwazi [Mvovo] and Beast [Mtawarira]. You don't really see a skin colour. You see a friend. I don't want to press my culture on other people. People have different visions.'

Dark-haired Bismarck has a brooding quality to him. He is less open, less extrovert than his blond brother. Unlike Jannie, who will balance his farm life with his medical career, Bismarck has only one love. Once his professional rugby-playing days are over, he will return to the family farms and there he will stay.

Even now, he regards the farm as his true home.

'We farm cattle and farm maize and beans and wheat.

'It's where I relax and switch off from everyday life. If someone is really looking for me, they phone my mom on the land line.'

He remains extremely close to his family, a closeness intensified by his father's illness. 'When my dad got sick, we really had to become closer-knit than other people, and a lot of the time growing up it felt like it was just me and Jannie and then my brother and sister.

'God always knew my dad would get sick, and we had the privilege of being kind of a father to our younger brother and sister, and my mom was there for all five of us. But it's heartbreaking. It's so difficult to watch his own frustration when he can't do things. My dad put everything he had into us two boys and one day, if I am privileged to have kids, I would like to be half the dad he was to me and Jannie.

'Growing up on a farm helps me in family values. It helped me to work hard because it is not a lifestyle where you can wake up and then have a leisurely breakfast. Work never stops, but it is very rewarding if you see your cow calving or your sheep giving birth and the pip you planted growing up. It keeps you on your knees. In the Bible there are many examples of farmers. You can compare yourself to what God saw.'

The biblical metaphors are strong in this family. I had mentioned to Jo-Helene how delightful Jannie's wedding had looked in the photographs: the setting was almost pantheistic. The ceremony was held outside with the golden sandstone cliffs and rocks forming a natural cathedral. The guests sat on bales of hay. But, as the service was getting going, there was a shower of rain and they all fled into the nearest shelter, a barn, where the ceremony resumed. Yes, said Jo-Helene, the pastor had remarked that Jesus was born in a barn in Bethlehem and now you're getting married in a barn in Bethlehem! Which I thought was rather charming.

Wolker, the farm manager, keeps things going while Bismarck and Jannie are in Durban, and Bismarck says 'I speak to him every day at 6am or 5.30 and he looks after my dad when there is trouble. It's like his farm.

'I wouldn't be able to live in the city. If I had three cows and a bit of maize, I'd be happy. Money is not something I live for. You need it to live but it's not something I run after. As long as I can provide for my family one day, that's all I want.'

Now, in Durban, he has a partnership in an insurance brokerage. Apparently, when Jannie first went to Durban to join Bismarck at the Sharks and they moved in together, he was somewhat demanding. Holding down his job at the hospital as well as playing rugby full-time, Jannie was irritated one day to find there was no toilet paper in the house. Bismarck was aggrieved to find himself landed with housekeeping chores. Get a job, advised his mother. Then you'll both be equally busy.

The insurance job keeps him humble, he says, and makes him appreciate rugby more.

'I could be sitting from eight to five in a 2- by 8m office and instead I run around in the sun and get to see places. I'm a focused guy when it comes to rugby and I love it, and it's really important that I do well, but, when I switch off, I really switch off.'

Life was about to take a bitter turn for him. A couple of days later, playing the Pumas at Newlands, he tore his cruciate ligament and was out for the rest of the year and for the start of the 2013 season. Adriaan Strauss took over as first-choice hooker and vice captain for the rest of the Rugby Championship and the end-of-year tour to Europe, winning lavish praise both for his performance on the field and for his leadership. Bismarck, meanwhile, struggled through an operation and months of tedious, painful rehabilitation.

Jannie played every game in both domestic and inter-national competitions: by the end of 2012, he had played 36 games, exceeding by four the upper limit of 32 games a year set by Sarpa, the players' union. He also kept his hospital job going and, in 2013, he became a father.

4 The Bok Captain

I live in Cape Town and am a regular at Newlands and at the Stormers' High Performance Centre in Bellville, so I have been able to build up an impression of Jean de Villiers over time. He is engaging and clearly very bright. And there is a deep humanity to the man.

Various conversations with him have produced a picture of a happy childhood. He was born with great advantages – good-looking, clever, a brilliant athlete – and life was initially an easy ride. He and his brother grew up with the kind of freedom that only a small-town setting and a secure, loving home can provide.

'I've been playing rugby since I was five years old,' he told me. 'There was a field nearby where everyone would gather to play touch rugby on Sundays, Mondays and Thursdays – all ages, from kids to older guys – and that was a great grounding for a backline player. Touch rugby teaches you to identify space around you and how to play into it.

'At weekends and in school holidays, I would leave the house at 8am with my tennis racquet and my rugby ball, and I would go on my bike to the primary school fields nearby, and I would stay there until six in the evening. My mom would give me R10 to buy a pie and a Coke for lunch and that was my life, day in and day out.'

For some kids, this kind of ease might have dulled the hunger necessary to achieve greatness. Apart from the contribution from his genes, there are probably two major factors that drove this particular kid on. The De Villiers family has deep roots: both parents were born and brought up in Paarl, but they have also lived through enormous changes in their immediate environment and their own place in it. The advent of black majority rule in 1994 required a decision by white people: they shrivelled away in the acid of their own bitterness, they packed for Perth, or they welcomed the changes and thrived. Which is what the De Villiers family has done. This kind of emotional resilience – the capacity to absorb challenges and emerge stronger – is a family trait. For almost two years of Jean's childhood, Nelson Mandela was living in a house in the grounds of the Victor Verster (now Drakenstein) prison, a few miles away from the De Villiers's home. It was from Paarl that Mandela walked the final few steps of his – and the nation's – long walk to freedom.

And then there was the way he was brought up. Both parents were equally engaged, but it was Louise who was the more hands-on. 'She is the one who always took us to athletics or swimming or cricket games or practices. My dad was quite busy working. He travelled a lot at that stage. He was the one I would go to for advice and just to know what it's about and the guy I looked up to.

'It was tough for my mom. She was outnumbered and we were not the easiest of boys. But she did have a massive part to play. And I'm very fortunate now that they can travel to a lot of my Test matches and games and they are still very involved and we see each other a lot.

'As a kid, I played everything. I swam provincially from the age of eight till sixteen. My mom still believes to this day that that was my best sport, but I'm more of a team guy and I enjoy a ball. Cricket was also a big game for me. I played first-team cricket for three years and captained the first team at school. Schalk and I played first-team cricket together. I played first-team rugby for two years.

'I did athletics at primary school but it was difficult to fit that in with rugby and cricket at high school. I did the biathlon provincially, which is athletics and swimming. So, I enjoyed sport. It was my life. I think I did get things easily. Even with my academics. I honestly didn't study much and I still got sixties and above without studying. I was pretty good at maths when I did study. But my brother was the clever one.'

His brother, Andre-Louis, now works at the short-term insurance company he, his father and Jean jointly own. He teaches the second rugby team at Paarl Gimnasium, his and Jean's alma mater. He too was heading for the rugby big-time until he injured his back and neck in a bad car accident. Prior to the accident, he and Jean played in the South African Under-19 team together. And Andre-Louis also played for the Western Province Under-21 team.

Jean, meanwhile, sprinted through all the key rugby milestones: he was chosen for the Craven Week Under-13 and Under-18 teams. With Andre-Louis, he played for the South African Under-19, Under-21 and Sevens teams.

He passed his final year with sufficiently high marks to get into Stellenbosch University. But, once there, he partied. 'We forced him to go to Stellenbosch because we thought it was important that he get a tertiary education,' says Louise. 'But he was wasting time and money. After six months at

Stellenbosch, we said to him: "What do you want to do with your life?" He said: "Play rugby." His dad said: "We will give you two years. If you make a success of it, you can carry on. Otherwise, you get an education.'"

And make a success of it he did. By the age of 21, he was a Springbok .

But then he hit his first major crisis. Six months after he became a Bok, Jean was badly injured.

'For the first time, I was in a situation where I had to work really hard to get back into the team and do my rehab to get back into playing again. I sometimes think those injuries and setbacks are good because they shake you up a bit and you realise what you need to do to be really successful.'

Two more devastating injuries put paid to his World Cup dreams. In 2003, he was injured in the last warm-up game before the team left for Australia. In the 2007 World Cup, he tore his biceps in the first game, against Samoa, and was out for the rest.

But, from each of these injuries, he came back stronger and more determined than ever, becoming the best player in his position in the world, his earlier sprinting prowess showing in explosive acceleration and a nimble mind and lightning reflexes producing some exhilarating intercept tries.

In 2010, he signed with Irish provincial side Munster. One of his reasons for choosing Ireland over a more lucrative contract with a French team was that there were no South Africans there. A rugby career is short, he told me, and he wanted to take as much from it as he could while he could – to grow as a person and learn skills he could take to his next job. Apart from his girlfriend, Marlie – now his wife – this

Afrikaans boy from Paarl removed himself from everything that was familiar. Stripped of his usual context, he must have had to look at himself anew. All his assumptions about himself and his place in the world must have been challenged.

He said the racial and linguistic diversity of Western Province helped him feel at home at Munster, where the team was made up of a motley bunch of nationalities – Irish, French, New Zealand and Australian. These differences fed the Irish '*craic*', or banter, which is what differentiates De Villiers today and makes him one of the journalists' favourites: he has a lovely dry wit which helps leaven press conferences.

After a year, Munster very much wanted him to stay on. But, at that point, Bok coach Peter de Villiers had said he would not select overseas-based players for the 2011 World Cup squad. And that was now Jean de Villiers's only goal: finally to play all the way through a World Cup. In the Springboks' opening game against Wales in the 2011 Rugby World Cup, he injured his rib cartilage, and I watched him roam up and down the edge of the field as the team played on without him. Dressed in the elegant, long green regulation Springbok coat against the biting wind, he cut a forlorn figure, so clearly desperate to be back on the field.

In the first game of the 2012 Super Rugby tournament, Stormers captain Schalk Burger injured his knee. De Villiers took over, shepherding a team with five 20-year-olds through to the top of the South African log. One of them, hooker Siyabonga Ntubeni, says that, on and off the field, De Villiers inspired: 'On the field, he never panics. He is always calm and he keeps the guys calm. Off-field, there was never the thing of "you're 20 and I'm a senior". From the moment

I started training with the team, he made me feel part of it. And he's good at the little things: he always makes sure we thank the bus driver. And, if we're at a restaurant and getting too boisterous, he will make us keep it down. And then thank the waiter and thank the manager.

'Some of the senior guys arrive late for gym sessions, but he is always the first to arrive and the last to leave. And, when fans are queuing up for autographs and photographs, other guys might slink off but Jean does every single one.'

When De Villiers, again injured, had to leave halfway through the Australasian leg of the 2012 Super Rugby campaign I thought that maybe part of him would be relieved. His first child had just been born. He must have been missing his family. Surely the pull of a more settled home life must be strong? But at the first press conference back in Cape Town, before the Stormers' game against the Cheetahs, for which he had been cleared to play, his elation was apparent. It's so hard, he said, to be sitting at home when the only place you want to be is on the field.

When the Stormers were once again ejected from the Super 15 in the 2012 semifinal, De Villiers showed an endearing vulnerability. 'When this keeps happening, you start looking deeply at what the real issue is. I'm starting to doubt myself and my captaincy,' he said, clearly upset.

Heyneke Meyer dismissed this bout of self-doubt, describing De Villiers as 'a brilliant captain'. 'What he said was just typical of him – he always looks at himself and blames himself first.'

For the then 31-year-old De Villiers, 2012 was a year of firsts. In June, he was anointed Springbok captain and again took on a bunch of youngsters, six of whom are twenty-two and under. Much of the senior cohort who had dominated the Bok team for the past few years had moved on, and much felt new. But there was also a sense of excitement, that this was a new beginning, a chance to start afresh after the debilitating 2011 Rugby World Cup.

'We are the bearers of the jersey now,' he said just before departing on the end-of-year European tour. 'And the team has grown a lot in the last few months. The guys are getting to know each other off the field and that carries through onto the field.'

One of the reasons Peter de Villiers hung onto John Smit for so long was that he was a unifying force. Within the Boks you had the powerful Bulls camp, the Sharks, the Stormers, all with different cultures, both on the field and off. Frequently, they had to play together shortly after dondering the hell out of each other the week before in a local derby. At that fateful World Cup quarterfinal in Wellington, South Africa fielded a team with 836 caps, which made it the most-capped starting line-up in Test history. In other words, a lot of very experienced men with their own ideas of how things should work. It took a very strong captain to get buy-in to the game plan from every single member of that squad.

Jean de Villiers has the same largeness of vision that Smit had. There is a scene in Smit's autobiography where All Blacks captain Richie McCaw expresses his surprise after overhearing a conversation between the then Bok captain and a British journalist. Smit had had to answer questions about 'apartheid, the quota system, whether there was a difference in captaining different cultures and races and what my views were regarding the status of rugby transformation in South Africa'. He said he realised then how different was his role from that of other international captains. 'I wouldn't change it for the world', he said. 'I truly believe it is our diversity that has made us a nation of survivors.'

Jean de Villiers shares Smit's political awareness and generosity of spirit. So I was surprised, during the Boks' 2012 end-of-year tour, to read a quote from De Villiers before the final England game, talking about the team needing to win in order to bring hope to South Africans, particularly at a time when there were 'bad and evil' things going on. It was most unlike De Villiers to buy into a sectarian narrative of moral slide and decay, and when he got back I asked him about this. Did he mean to be critical? Not at all, he said vehemently. The context was that the farm workers' strike was going on at the time, and vivid images of violence and destruction were filling British TV screens and newspapers. You know how they always play up the bad stuff, he said. It pained him, to see this kind of suffering. 'It's people's livelihoods.' And he felt an additional responsibility to his fellow South Africans to bring them a bit of cheer that Saturday by winning.

And win they did, against all the odds.

Sitting beside him on the bench at the High Performance Centre, watching the forwards go over their line-outs one more time, I ask him: What makes a great Bok?

He answers immediately: 'The guy who puts the Springbok first. Talent alone won't make you a great Bok. You get a lot of guys for whom it's not special. But not a lot of people get that opportunity, and you have to do everything in your ability to help the team; whether you are sitting in the stands, on the bench or starting, your commitment must always be the same. That is what marks a great Bok from an average one. With that goes hard work, the respect of your peers and supporters. Not only on the field but also off it, and, wherever you go, you need to make being a Springbok someone people can look up to.

'There is no other way – you have to do it 100%. You have to give everything for the team. That to me is the great thing about rugby – you depend on the team so much. You need every single oke in that team to be pulling in the same direction, otherwise it's not going to work.

'You get a lot of guys who don't get the opportunity; they are on four consecutive tours and they don't play one game, yet they are still so committed to the cause and they keep the vibe up in the squad. They know their role within the team and still contribute, even though they might not be playing that Saturday.'

Would you pick that kind of person before one who is pure talent and less of a team player, I ask.

'You need balance,' he replies. 'Ideally you need both talent and commitment. In every player you need that package. Sometimes you will go for the guy who is less talented and contributes more in the other departments. That is the beauty of a team sport.'

As a leader, you need to understand each player and how to get the best from him. 'You will be spending more time with some guys than others. Last year, we created a happy culture and the guys seemed to enjoy it and we managed to pull games together and win games through guts and commitment.'

He talks about the highlights of the Boks' 2012: 'In the Aussie game at Loftus, we just clicked and everything went well for us. The first game against England, too, my first as captain. Everything went well for us. And I scored that try. And then that second test against England in Joburg – the first 30 minutes, I felt unbeatable. Just everything went right for us. We played some amazing rugby. The score didn't really reflect the dominance we had earlier in that game.'

But the ultimate 2012 game for him in terms of sheer team spirit and triumph over adversity was the final win over England at Twickenham.

'We didn't play the way we wanted to, and we can still improve on that a lot from a technical and tactical point of view, but the commitment that was shown ... that's something you can't coach. That comes from within and shows the guys are playing for something bigger than the individual.

'It shows what the country means. For me, the end-of-year of tour, there was so much going on. The grape-pickers' strike – for three and a half weeks. You aren't here experiencing everything and you see all the bad news all the time. And you feel you need to give hope. When you're abroad, it makes it worse than it really is because you only get the bad news. That makes me sad and I think it makes the responsibility more for us – it puts greater pressure on us to just win. Because if the Boks lose again ...

'The relief at the end of that England game! Because it was on a knife's edge. And for the coach as well. If we'd lost that one, it would have been a 50% win ratio. Winning it meant we won 7 out of 12. So we only lost three – against the top three teams in the world at that stage. Seven out of 12 was a pass and hopefully we can keep on improving on that.'

De Villiers predicts a good 2013 for the Boks 'and that is due to grinding out wins last year and putting things in place'.

'I'd love to still be here – if I'm good enough, hopefully I can.'

Later, I asked Heyneke Meyer the same question: which was the most satisfying game of 2012? He agreed with De Villiers: it was that last England game.

'I have never seen players that tired. It was a very inexperienced side, most of whom had never played in England before. Every player was carrying a minor injury.

'The crowd got behind England. It was one of the best defensive efforts I have ever seen from the team. What for me was a real compliment was that England went for poles because they knew how good our defence was.'

Trailing South Africa 16-12 with three minutes left, England were awarded a penalty. Having lost narrowly to Australia the week before, England captain Chris Robshaw opted to kick for goal. South Africa won by a single point.

'Mentally, we could build on that,' says Meyer. 'You win the World Cup with great defences. The whole tour was great because we had an unbelievable vibe. Jean has grown a lot as captain and he kept the guys together.'

There was an interesting statistic here: on tour, both South Africa and New Zealand allocate a single room to every player with more than 50 caps. The others have to share two to a room. 'New Zealand had 16 guys in single rooms. We had two,' says Meyer.

'Experience can absorb pressure. The players played for each other.'

The conditions were awful, and were new to most of the

players. Most of the game was played in icy, drenching rain. 'The whole week, we trained in icy conditions. Our slogan for that week was: "We don't get bad weather. We only get soft players." I couldn't speak because my lips were numb.' But they trained on, the big freeze notwithstanding. 'From training, they got used to the conditions.'

The victory was all the more sweet because England ostensibly had the upper hand. They are used to performing in cold conditions. They were playing at their home ground and they had the crowd behind them.

And the very same England side went on to score five tries against the All Blacks the following week, decisively beating the first-ranked team in the world.

Meyer believes that England will be the team to watch in the 2015 World Cup. They will again have home-ground advantage and familiar conditions.

De Villiers, meanwhile, came back into 2013 injury-free and fighting fit. And confirmed as Springbok captain for another year.

5 The Coaches

When asked who their most influential coach was, Springboks frequently point to their first coach. And so it was that, in Bethlehem one freezing night, I found myself clutching the outstretched hand of a blind man and bowing my head in prayer.

Jannie and Bismarck du Plessis's first coach was one Marius Grobler, the blind man in whose kitchen I am sitting, about to tuck into the meal we have jointly asked God to bless. Marius Grobler lives with his wife, Helene, in a quiet suburb north of Bethlehem's busy main road. Attached to the house are the consulting rooms in which he practises his new vocation: healing.

I had arranged to meet Grobler there at 5pm after the day's healing was done. He comes out to greet me, led by his guide dog, a Labrador named Yukon. In the lounge, Grobler eases himself into an armchair directly opposite me: what little sight he has left is tunnel vision. Yukon sinks into the dog basket beside him. Every now and again, Grobler reaches over to stroke the dog, and he keeps the lead firmly gripped in his right hand.

I explain my mission: that I want to understand the formative influences on the Du Plessis brothers' lives in order to crack the formula to producing great Springboks.

Grobler was the woodwork teacher at Truida Kestell primary school, to which both Jannie and Bismarck were sent as weekly boarders from the age of six. As was the case in those days of universally multi-tasking teachers, he also coached the under-9 A rugby team and was housemaster at the hostel, where he assumed a surrogate father role to the two little Du Plessis boys during the week.

Tentatively, I ask about his sight: did this not make his job difficult? He tells me that it wasn't until 2001, well after the boys had left Truida Kestell, that he began to experience difficulties. The diagnosis was retinitis pigmentosa, an eye disease that causes damage to the retina. It is incurable and results in progressively deteriorating vision. By 2006, he had had to give up the job he loved.

I ask him what the boys were like at school, and he smiles.

'Bismarck was the naughtiest boy I have ever taught. He was always playing tricks on the other kids, or brawling. He was a very strong kid, coming from the farm, and he had Jannie as his big brother. But a boy needs to be naughty, and, if he did something wrong, he would always admit it and take his punishment.' Punishment in those days, of course, meant a caning.

Grobler was Jannie's and Bismarck's first coach, and their only coach throughout primary school, moving up with them from the under-9s to the under-13s.

Truida Kestell produced not only the Du Plessis brothers but also Francois Steyn, whom Grobler also coached. 'Right from the beginning, I knew these two guys would be Springboks: Bismarck and Frans.'

When Jannie was old enough to play in the under-9 A team, Bismarck hung around the edge of the field, desperate to be in a team with the big boys. Until they were old enough to play in the under-9s, kids played unstructured rugby without line-outs or scrums. 'He didn't like that. He was always saying: "Sir, I want to play the real game!"'

'One day, there was a touring side from Durban and one of our guys didn't pitch up so I said, "Bismarck, do you want to play?" I slotted him in as fullback. He was such a natural. He was only seven and playing for the under-9s and he was great. He tackled and he bled and he cried but he went on and on. This tiny guy with the big heart.

'He never got the ball but he tackled and tackled and tackled, even though he was way smaller than the others. They used to play for 15 minutes a side so he tackled for 30 minutes. And we won.

'We kept quiet about it because you weren't allowed to play underage players but it was at that game that I saw the potential in this guy.'

Whenever the team went on tour after that, Bismarck accompanied them and trained with them, even though his age still sidelined him from the match itself.

The following year, both boys played in the under-9 team, the first time they had played together in a team.

One can see why Marius, in particular, had such a strong influence on Bismarck. They lived together from Monday to Friday, and on Saturdays they came together again to play rugby. Living in the hostel made rugby – and Marius – even more central to the boys' lives, entailing as it did incessant spontaneous practice.

'Rugby was the big game. If there was a ball, they would play rugby. They used to play after dinner and it was the Grade 1s to Grade 7s all together and they played hard. There was almost no grass and there you really got to see what they were like. It was in those after-dinner games that I saw it in Bismarck: this guy's a hooker. From under-9, he was hooker.

'So we all moved up to under-11s and I was again their coach. So two years in each age team and Bismarck always played in the A team.'

From the beginning, Bismarck was a confrontational, aggressive player. Marius gives an example of a game against Ficksburg. Bismarck was in the under-13 A team, even though he was only twelve. 'He got the ball, and there was about 30m he had to run to the tryline and there was a wing about twenty paces to the right, so he could have veered off, but he went straight for the guy, ran over him and then scored the try.'

Another hallmark was the boy's sense of commitment. 'For instance, if his mom said to him, "You are sick. You can't go to practice," he would sneak off to practice. There was just no way he would miss it, even if it meant being punished for disobedience.

'In the off-season, he would tie a rope around an old tyre and drag it behind him, to build up his strength. At home, their dad had built them an obstacle course and Bismarck kept asking me for one. So I asked his dad and he built another one at the school. After that, whenever you looked for Bismarck, that is where he would be. Then his dad came to me and asked if he could install a pole with a basket that could be moved up and down so that Bismarck could practise his line-out throw and vary it between the number 4 and number 6. Once that was up, that was where Bismarck would be. In season, practice was between four and five but he would be there early. And that is amazing for an eleven-year-old.'

Marius believes that Bismarck is a natural Springbok captain. His leadership qualities, he says, were evident from the beginning.

'There were a few chubby guys in the group, so I looked for the fittest four or five and asked them to run with these guys and push them and push them till they became fit. Every day, he was there chasing those guys. That is also the leadership you are seeing in Biz now. That was in Grade 7 that he was showing this kind of leadership.

'From under-13 A, he was my captain and that was the year that he got his northern Free State colours in rugby. It was also the first year we won the eastern Free State league. And, in our area, the competition is big.'

It's not something I'm used to, having an intense conversation with an almost blind man, and I keep forgetting he can't really see me. So I apologise as I put on my coat, worrying that he will see it as a comment on his hospitality – it's after dark and the temperature has dropped to below zero. There is one heater, but the room is chilly. He doesn't say anything, and it quickly occurs to me: he didn't have to know. Another time I make a reference to something on TV and then metaphorically kick myself: how stupid! But he reacts to none of it. This is clearly a man who has come to terms with his disability and asks no favours for it.

Yukon slumbers peacefully at his side, his comfort zone. The other source of comfort is his wife, Helene, who comes in every now and then with refreshments: tea when I arrive, a glass of red wine at 6pm, an invitation to stay for dinner at 7pm. It's a long conversation and I'm enjoying it. As is Marius.

It is clearly immensely gratifying to him that his charges have done so brilliantly. He remains close not only to the Du Plessis family but also to Frans Steyn's parents. The right parents, he says, were a crucial component in the making of these Boks.

'The parents were always there for them, always doing their best for their children, and that is what a child needs. I used to get a lot of parents just pushing and pushing, and if the team loses it is always the coach's fault.

'Francois [du Plessis] was the opposite: he would come and ask me what he could do to help. He devised a scrumming machine attached to a tractor and he would bring that in from the farm for the boys to practise on. A whole scrummaging machine! Francois would sit on the tractor and manoeuvre the thing up and down so they could simulate scrumming. He made it so great, and those boys loved scrumming from early days. We scrummed the other guys into the ground every time.

'He never pushed; always just helped.'

And not only his own children. Just up the hill from Truida Kestell is a children's home, situated between the primary school and Voortrekker High, which is on the crest of the hill. The orphans were absorbed into each school.

'There were always orphans in our team, and Jo-Helene and Francois made sure they had the clothes they needed and the transport. And the boys were the same.

'Francois is a very gentle, giving person. He will give you anything. He will put everything aside to help. We became such good friends over the years. And they are such a close family. They and the Steyns are the closest families I have ever seen in my coaching career, and it just turns out that all three became Springboks.

'With both the Steyns and the Du Plessis parents, if things were not going well, they would say to the kids: "Don't worry. *Môre is nog 'n dag.*" Not pushing, pushing, like the other parents.'

It's important to teach kids balance, he says.

'You must teach them that life is not just about winning. Sometimes you will lose, and the parents must stay with you when you are losing. That is what a good parent does: he stays with them in loss as well. Some parents, when we lose, blame the ref or the coach or say the kid didn't play to his full potential. So, if we lose, it is someone else to blame. But, if we win, they are with you all the way.

'The third Du Plessis son, Tabbi, is not so good at sport but he is such a nice bloke. Tabbi might think: my two brothers are Springboks so where do I fit in? People might think he would not get the sunlight. It takes a very special family to get that right.

'As a teacher, you pick this up very quickly. I'm mad about sport, but my daughter, my only child, is not very sporty, but I try to be like the Du Plessis parents. I say to her: you don't need to be in the A team or the B team. Just take part.'

Bismarck might have had the superior athletic talent, but it was Jannie who starred academically.

'Biz struggled in the lower grades. He would always rather play than study but look at him now – you wonder if his teachers up till Grade 7 would think he would have a university degree.'

It was in Grade 7 that Bismarck started to show an interest in girls for the first time. 'He was always having a go at the girls. Until Grade 7. Then it all changed.'

To Jannie, schoolwork came easily. 'When Jannie was in Grade 7, I introduced a system in the hostel whereby guys who got over 90% could study in the dormitory. They didn't have to go to the study hall with the others. Jannie was the first to win that privilege.'

Helene calls us in to supper. Spread out on the kitchen table are steaming dishes of chicken, potatoes, carrots, cabbage and peas. Marius, led by Yukon, takes his place at the head of the table. With my wine topped up, I am about to tuck into the fragrant pile in front of me when Marius calls a halt, stretching one hand out to his wife and the other to me. We bow our heads and pray.

∗ ∗ ∗

Jean de Villiers's first coach was Vis Waso. He was no longer in touch with him, he said. But his parents were, and Louise kindly supplied me with his phone number.

Vis Waso, like Marius Grobler, turned out to be a humble, unpretentious man, and quite overwhelmed at the prospect of being interviewed about his famous protégé. I arrive first at the meeting place he suggested: one of Paarl's many stylish little cafés. Vis arrives, a tall, lean man in chinos and a red pullover.

He is very modest and can't imagine what he could possibly add to any portrait of his most famous product. He is not confident of his English – and I am not confident of my Afrikaans – so we proceed with my asking questions in English and Vis replying in Afrikaans and we understand each other very well.

Vis was Jean's first and only coach from pre-primary school to under-13. Like Marius Grobler, he was also a primary school teacher and, in Grade 7, he taught Jean maths, Afrikaans and geography.

Vis says he realised at once that he was dealing with an exceptional talent. From a very early age, Jean would analyse his game. 'He has vision. He can instantly sum up a situation. Even as a kid, he was recognised as a game-maker and targeted by the opposition. From under-13, they would try to injure him – for instance, with late tackles. But he always came back. He never let them get away with it.'

And, even though he knew he had talent, he worked very hard. 'Jean always gave more than 100%. He put everything into it: not just into rugby, but into swimming, athletics and cricket. He is a natural player, make no mistake. But he is a player who has always given his all.'

This is an important point: his work ethic. 'You get kids who have lots of talent but don't try,' says Vis. They don't make it through to the big-time either.

Jean was also a leader. 'He got lots of respect from his team-mates and he was always my captain: for two years in the under-12s and two years in the under-13s. He was streets ahead of the others.'

Vis does not approve of the type of rugby the Bok backline is made to play now. It was not what he taught his prodigy. 'There is no creativity! I did not coach structured rugby. A kid must just play. Until he was 13, Jean played according to his instinct.' All he wants is to see this again, at the highest level. 'Let him play his natural game. They will get a fright at what they see.'

He sighs. 'I haven't seen another kid like him: with that talent and that commitment. He has a magical touch.'

* * *

It was under Heyneke Meyer that Jean de Villiers was to achieve his full potential as leader when Meyer appointed him Springbok captain on the eve of the British and Irish Lions Tour of 2012.

Shortly after Heyneke's appointment as Springbok head coach at the beginning of 2012, I set out to interview him at his base in Pretoria. I was coming in from Johannesburg on the Gautrain, and Heyneke and De Jongh Borchardt, his media manager, had offered to pick me up from Pretoria's Hatfield station.

The Gautrain bus drivers are on strike, so there are several of us milling around in the morning sunshine waiting for lifts. Some take the opportunity for a quick smoke; others chat on cellphones. I wander around the block, not going too far in case I miss their arrival, marvelling at the bright, spacious station, the generous concourse and the winding concrete layers of the car park opposite. The train ride in from Joburg has been swift, efficient, scenic. It was just as good as any European railway network, without the crowds and the grime. I am worrying briefly about this – how will it sustain itself when it is so empty at this, the rush hour? – when I feel a tap on my shoulder.

It's De Jongh, breathing heavily because, as he explains, they've parked on the other side of the station, at the entrance to the car park, and he's had to hurry up the ramp and through the concourse to find me. I follow him back through the station to where Heyneke is sitting in the passenger seat of a modest white sedan. He holds up a hand in greeting and continues chatting on his cell. He's doing an interview with an Afrikaans radio station. De Jongh and I sit there in silence for a few minutes while Heyneke rounds off his conversation, and then he tells De Jongh he can drive and simultaneously wheels around to face me. He switches off his phone and I get his full, high-wattage focus.

Heyneke Meyer, in this, the honeymoon, phase of his tenure as Springbok coach, radiates a messianic zeal. His grey hair is well cut and neatly combed; his blue striped cotton shirt crisp and spotless. It is not yet 9am and he's already had a busy morning. His wife, Linda, is off on a three-week mountaineering trip in South America. They had had a brief conversation by satellite phone the night before – their only means of contact. He, meanwhile, is caring for their three sons, the youngest of whom is only ten. He has already fed them, supervised their homework and taken them to school. The oldest, though, is now a boarder at Affies. At home, says Heyneke, the domestic worker picks up after him. In the hostel, he will have to learn to look after himself. What I gather from all this is that he is an engaged, modern father and that this is a high-achieving, driven family. Linda's PhD included some ground-breaking research into the commercial growing of mushrooms and she has been teaching in the Department of Microbiology and Plant Pathology at the

University of Pretoria. She has had a bout with cancer but has conquered it and is about to start her own business.

As we talk, De Jongh pilots us vigorously through downtown Pretoria. After about ten minutes, we pull into a parking lot in a suburban shopping centre and Heyneke leads me into a coffee shop. I follow him through the crowded tables and up a flight of stairs to a small mezzanine level. There is one other person there, a woman working on a laptop, but the chatter from below rises through a flimsy balustrade.

We sit down at a corner table and order coffees. Heyneke has yet to finalise his contract. It is 16 February 2012, three weeks since SARU announced to a delighted rugby community that he was the new South African national coach. But they've got themselves into exactly the same position as they did with Peter de Villiers: publicly declaring their commitment to him before he's signed off on his to them.

The difficulties now are over his management team. He is very clear about whom he wants. 'I can tell you now that I'm going to get a lot of bad press because I'm going to pick guys who are not well known. I'm going to pick guys from the Bulls. Most of the best coaches are at the Bulls: I know because I've spent ten years getting them in. The national team should have the best coaches. If you don't get the best people around you, you will be struggling.'

He has worked with these coaches through several successful campaigns, so they are all on the same page. They share his vision. And this is crucial, given the very brief amount of time they will have to work together to prepare the team before the first Test – against England in June.

It won't be easy. The Bulls are understandably reluctant to

release what is the core of their own coaching staff. There will be intense negotiations. And expensive transfer fees. 'It's going to be hectic.'

The last time I spent any time with Heyneke was at a marathon three-hour session in his office at Loftus in early 2010. He had just rejoined the Bulls after a year in the UK coaching the Leicester Tigers. I'd been impressed with the determination with which he'd eradicated the failing Bulls culture he'd inherited at the turn of the century and built a winning one.

He is approaching this job with the same energy and determination. He believes he knows what kind of team he needs to make South Africa the number-one rugby nation in the world. And what he needs to do to build it.

I ask him who his captain will be. For the past four years, Schalk Burger has been the name on many lips. 'Schalk has been captain of Province, but so what? There are five other captains. Surely he should have been made captain mid-week? Or they should have made him captain in friendlies to give him the exposure.'

There are two things here that strike me as likeable about Heyneke Meyer: firstly, that his ego is not attached to pomp. The simplicity of this meeting place, the small car, the offer to come and fetch me rather than making me come to him: it all speaks of a man sure of himself, one who does not need excessive trappings and flunkeys to inflate his importance.

The other aspect I like is his openness. He answers all my questions fully and conscientiously. And, I feel, honestly. One gets the sense of a man whose emotions are close to the surface. There is no dissimulation.

I explain the theme of my book and he gives me his view, which is that you have to get them young. Potential Springbok captains, for instance. 'You should be looking at the under-20 captains every year so that you have four or five guys in the picture. You should send them on courses: how to work with the media, how to deal with finances, how to be presentable, leadership skills. These guys are nineteen and twenty, so when someone like John Smit moves on you have a guy who has been ready for five years.'

Heyneke is a great believer in starting from the bottom up: finding decent, malleable raw material and moulding it. He quotes from *Outliers* by Malcolm Gladwell, and in particular from the first chapter, 'The Matthew Effect'. Gladwell uses the example of Canadian ice hockey to show the crucial difference made by good coaching. Ice hockey in Canada, he points out, is deeply democratic. Most boys are taught at school from an early age. It was a Canadian psychologist named Roger Barnsley who first drew attention to the edge provided by age and what this meant in terms of long-term success. Barnsley's research showed that, in any elite squad of hockey players, 40% will have been born between January and March, 30% between April and June, 20% between July and September and 10% between October and December.

Later I read Gladwell, who sums up his conclusions thus: 'In Canada, the eligibility cut-off for age-class hockey is January 1. A boy who turns ten on January 2, then, could be playing alongside someone who doesn't turn ten until the end of the year – and at that age, in pre-adolescence, a 12-month gap in age represents an enormous difference in physical maturity.'

Ice hockey, like rugby, is a contact sport, so bigger and

stronger is good. Like rugby for certain sections of the South African population, Canadians are passionate about ice hockey. Scouts start looking for boys for elite travelling squads from the ages of nine or ten and tend to favour those who are bigger and better coordinated. A boy born early in the year will have benefited from critical extra months of physical maturity.

Once a boy has been absorbed into an elite squad, points out Gladwell, 'he gets better coaching; his team-mates are better, and he plays fifty or seventy-five games a season instead of twenty games a season like those left behind in the "house" league, and he practices twice as much as, or even three times more than he would have otherwise. In the beginning, his advantage is not so much that he is inherently better but only that he is a little older. But by the age of thirteen or fourteen, with the benefit of better coaching and all that extra practice under his belt, he really is better, so he's the one more likely to make it to the Major Junior A league, and from there into the big leagues.'

Sitting beside me in the Pretoria coffee shop, Meyer tells me that his own experience bears out Gladwell's theories. In virtually every case and on every level, he says, the extent to which a player will flourish depends on the input he receives: 'In every team, there are three or four superstars. But, other than that, in every position, there is nothing to choose between the top ten players. It's just a matter of giving the right guy the right coaching structure. And then, what I'm big on is the character: that is what makes the difference. You see these guys coming in every year and you see who makes it and who doesn't. The talent base is the same.'

The right guy means the guy with the right character. 'Character is like a piece of charcoal: it costs nothing, but if you put enough pressure on a piece of charcoal over the years, you get a diamond. I like certain players because of their character. If I take a number 10 and give him more coaching and more life skills than the other guy, he will surpass him.'

He's animated, eyes shining, clearly happy to expound on a theory close to his heart. What does he define as character, I ask. He answers immediately with a phrase I hear a lot over the months to come.

'Mental toughness. After three playing sessions, I can tell you which player will make it and which not. After tough sessions, guys who walk out and sit out will always sit out when it's tough. You also look at their upbringing. When I'm recruiting youngsters ... now, how do I put this sensitively? ... You can get youngsters from the boys' schools. They've got their own hostel, they are put under pressure from the seniors, there are no parents around.'

So that's why his own son is in the hostel, despite the fact that the family lives in Pretoria.

'When I recruit youngsters, the father will sit here, the mother will sit here, and the kid will sit here,' he says, pointing at each of the four chairs at our table in turn. 'Now, 90% of the time the mother will want boarding; the washing must be done and they must study. The father just wants him to play rugby. He doesn't care. You get kids who, in an hour's conversation, don't say a word. The parents speak for them the whole hour. I want to hear from him: what does he want to do? What is his dream? But clearly he is a youngster who can't express himself. He's been overwhelmed his whole life. He's never been able to fight for himself.

'But it's not only that – he must also have integrity; he must have a good work ethic; if they've had things easy all their lives and suddenly there are ten superstars and they have to train very, very hard to compete, they just don't go further. But a guy who doesn't have other options, a never-say-die attitude, and he works for the guy next to him – that is the big difference.'

De Jongh interrupts us: Heyneke has a meeting at the SuperSport offices in Randburg and they need to leave now if he is to be on time. Come along for the ride, they say to me.

I sit in the back seat and Heyneke in the passenger seat while De Jongh drives. I ask Heyneke why he thinks we lost to Australia in the Rugby World Cup, but he doesn't want to comment on anything that happened during another coach's tenure. He is happy, however, to talk about the threat posed by the team that inflicted that devastating defeat on us. Twisting further round in the passenger seat so that he can face me full on, he expounds on his early theory, that it all goes back to the early years.

'Some 80% of Springboks and SA Schools players come out of ten schools: they have the best coaching, the best work ethic; they've got a rugby culture. Where Aussie gets it right is that they don't have a big player base because most of their guys go to league and other footie games, but the guys who do play union get quality coaching and quality facilities. And so I believe the reason we are falling behind in coaching in South Africa is that there are no more coaching courses. What I would like to do is to bring experts from around the world and bring them into the coaching structures.'

In Australia, not only is rugby played at private schools with ample resources, but the state also pumps money into academies that take player preparation one step further. They have a world-class sports science body, in the form of the Australian Institute of Sport. South Africa, with its many more pressing demands on the public fiscus, clearly can't afford the same level of engagement. So we need to find ways round it.

'That is why I would like to be director of coaching so I can do this kind of thing: develop captains, spend time with the top coaches and put them through courses.

'Our top ten schools are not elite enough – they are mostly public, not private schools as in Australia. In South Africa, we can't put money into sport; we need housing and other basic things. It's about money – if you look at how much money Australia puts into sport and how much we do, you can't compare. If you look at the smaller unions here, that is why they can't compete. At the Bulls, I had a kicking coaching, a scrumming coach, a conditioning coach – they don't have money for that. So they will never catch up.'

We've arrived at the SuperSport offices. It's a symbiotic relationship this: SuperSport is effectively the marketing arm of SA Rugby. Underlining the importance of the relationship, today's workshop is one of the first Heyneke will give.

The first person we bump into in the car park is Naas Botha. He and Heyneke greet each briefly. Then Bob Skinstad. There's Owen Nkumane, Xola Ntshinga, Ashwin Willemse – all hurrying in through SuperSport's narrow reception area. It's 10am and the workshop is about to start. Victor Matfield, the newest recruit to the SuperSport stable, is already waiting. Like the others, he is dressed in a pale blue cotton shirt, with the tails elegantly trailing. They all head through to the studio: a new coach, a new presentation to work out. A new goal to work towards: bringing home the Webb Ellis Cup in 2015.

It is during a quiet period in the 2011 World Cup campaign that I got my first glimpse into how fraught things had become for Heyneke's predecessor, Peter de Villiers. After the second of the pool games, against Fiji, the Springbok camp had moved to Taupo, a resort town in the centre of the North Island. Taupo is situated on a geological fault line, which means that there is a constant build-up of boiling water underground. Every so often, the earth emits a low growl, which indicates an urgent need to let off steam, and council workers arrive to drill holes into the ground. The Bayview Wairakei Resort, where the Boks – and I – are staying is ringed by a river of hot water, and plumes of steam escape from spots in the hotel grounds. Rocks are packed around each hole so that unsuspecting guests do not accidentally step into one and boil their feet.

The hotel itself is perfectly pleasant. The Bayview is 8km from Taupo and the rooms are spread out over several hectares, with beautiful lawns and flowers and trees, all bursting with spring blossom. There is none of the claustrophobia of our previous billet, the Wellington InterContinental, with its single exit and entrance, clogged with fans.

But the build-up of steam, periodically bursting out into the open, is an apt metaphor for what is going on inside the hotel.

I am having a glass of wine in the bar one evening with

a colleague when Peter de Villiers stops by our table. We invite him to join us.

He's got to take care of something but he'll be back, he says. And, sure enough, half an hour later, he arrives. With an entourage: Craig Roberts, the team doctor, and Malome Maimane, the technical analyst, a warm man with a smile that could light up a room but with a mind that ticks with endless statistics.

We settle down with more drinks. Peter de Villiers sticks to ginger ale. As the evening progresses and the others peel off to bed, he grows more confiding and I begin to understand for the first time quite how dramatic is the balancing act required of a Springbok coach. He says that, even if he succeeds in becoming the first coach to retain the Webb Ellis Cup, his career with the Boks is at an end. Peter is an angry man.

'I am the only coach in the world who has not been offered a new contract,' he says. 'The only one in the world! I have researched it.' His contract expires on 31 December, no matter what happens in New Zealand. Jurie Roux, the SARU CEO, is staying in the hotel with us. Potential relief from his anxiety about his future could not be at closer quarters. Yet, so far, it is not forthcoming.

He must give all to this crucial campaign, not knowing what will happen to him when it is over.

What he would like, he says, is at least another year in which he can help bed in a new coach. The new man would make the decisions, he says. But he, Peter, would be there to impart what he has learnt, for his successor to build on. But, even at this eleventh hour, there is no offer on the table.

It seems to me there is a startling disjuncture between the man's apparent power and the shaky foundations upon which it rests. He is king for now. But, by the end of the year, he could be a nobody. He will not beg for a job, he says. He went through all that the first time round and will never do it again.

He recalls the drama and struggle that surrounded his appointment. SARU made the mistake of announcing his appointment before he had signed the contract. They tried to get him to accept less than what Jake White had earned and he refused to sign, holding out until he was offered the same conditions as Jake had. He also secured the right to the final say over selection.

He talks about the blight cast on his tenure from the beginning by Oregan Hoskins, recalling the exact words the SARU president used. They are obviously burnt into his mind: 'I want to be honest with South Africa and say that the appointment was not entirely made for rugby reasons. We have made the appointment and taken into account the issue of transformation when we made it.' 'What hurt me the most,' he says, 'was that he comes from the same background as me.' Another coloured man. 'That was very painful.'

And this lack of support continued. 'He never supported me over that videotape business.' He is referring to an attempt to blackmail him in 2008 over a videotape that allegedly showed De Villiers in a compromising position with a woman who was not his wife.

The appointment of De Villiers was, in fact, a good example of the problems within SARU. They had two other eminently suitable candidates: Heyneke Meyer and Allister

The coach, his captain and the minister: Heyneke Meyer and Jean de Villiers flank Sports Minister Fikile Mbalula, in the gardens of the Montecasino Hotel, 5 October 2012. The promising young Springbok flyhalf, Johan Goosen, looks on. The unlucky 20-year-old was to sustain a season-ending knee injury during the game against the All Blacks that day.

Proportion of rugby-playing schools by province

Source: Sports Science Institute of SA research (2012) against schools data for 2010

Schools producing 3 or more Springboks
(source: www.genslin.us)

16%
GAUTENG

- 🎽 6 Hoërskool Monument, Krugersdorp
- 🎽 5 Afrikaanse Hoër Seunskool, Pretoria
- 🎽 3 Pretoria Boys High
- 🎽 3 Hoërskool Waterkloof, Pretoria

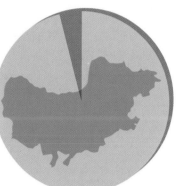

4%
NORTH WEST

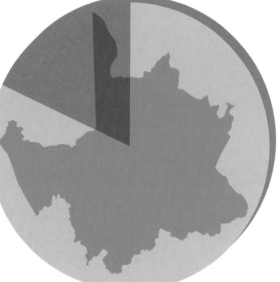

18%
NORTHERN CAPE

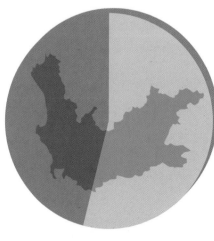

46%
WESTERN CAPE

- 🎽 10 Paarl Gimnasium
- 🎽 6 Diocesan College, Cape Town (Bishops)
- 🎽 6 Paul Roos Gymnasium, Stellenbosch
- 🎽 3 Boland Landbou, Paarl
- 🎽 3 Hoër Landbouskool Oakdale, Riversdal

2%
LIMPOPO

3%
MPUMALANGA

🎽 Hoërskool Nelspruit,
Mbombela

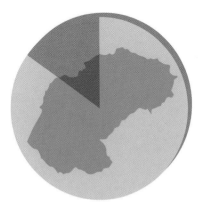

15%
FREE STATE
🎽 Grey College, Bloemfontein
🎽 Hoërskool Kroonstad (Blouskool)
🎽 Hoërskool Sand du Plessis, Bloemfontein

3%
KWAZULU-NATAL
🎽 Durban High School
🎽 Hilton College
🎽 Maritzburg College
🎽 Northwood School, Durban

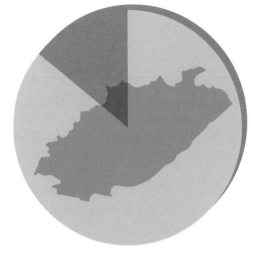

14%
EASTERN CAPE
🎽 Selborne College, East London
🎽 Adelaide Gimnasium, Piet Retief
🎽 Dale College, King William's Town
🎽 Queen's College, Queenstown

Total rugby-playing schools and clubs by province
*Sports Science Institute of SA research (2012)

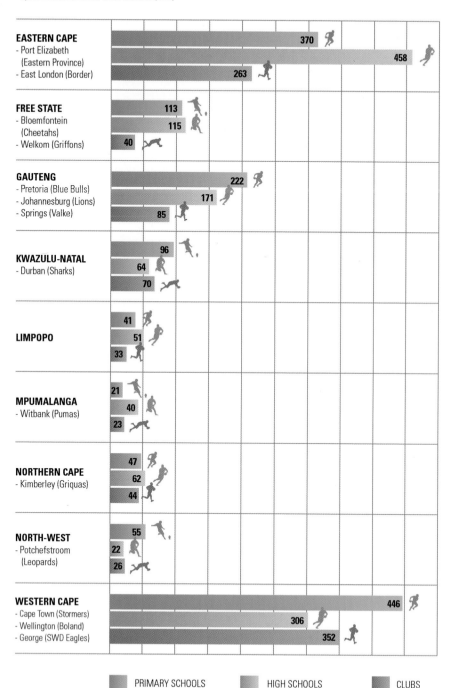

EASTERN CAPE
- Port Elizabeth
  (Eastern Province)
- East London (Border)

370
458
263

FREE STATE
- Bloemfontein
  (Cheetahs)
- Welkom (Griffons)

113
115
40

GAUTENG
- Pretoria (Blue Bulls)
- Johannesburg (Lions)
- Springs (Valke)

222
171
85

KWAZULU-NATAL
- Durban (Sharks)

96
64
70

LIMPOPO

41
51
33

MPUMALANGA
- Witbank (Pumas)

21
40
23

NORTHERN CAPE
- Kimberley (Griquas)

47
62
44

NORTH-WEST
- Potchefstroom
  (Leopards)

55
22
26

WESTERN CAPE
- Cape Town (Stormers)
- Wellington (Boland)
- George (SWD Eagles)

446
306
352

PRIMARY SCHOOLS   HIGH SCHOOLS   CLUBS

SARU budget 2012: Income

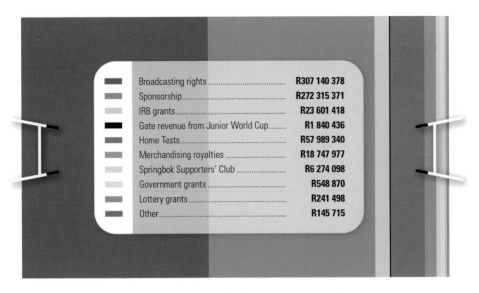

Broadcasting rights	R307 140 378
Sponsorship	R272 315 371
IRB grants	R23 601 418
Gate revenue from Junior World Cup	R1 840 436
Home Tests	R57 989 340
Merchandising royalties	R18 747 977
Springbok Supporters' Club	R6 274 098
Government grants	R548 870
Lottery grants	R241 498
Other	R145 715

TOTAL: R688 845 101

SARU budget 2012: Operations

Commercial and marketing	R231 593 599
High performance	R149 269 660
Allocations to provinces	R140 623 798
Development	R68 478 559
Human resources	R5 066 212
Corporate affairs	R12 279 956
Referees	R34 199 219
Operations and finance	R31 461 472
CEO's office	R8 844 510
Governance	R10 712 136
Springbok Supporters' Club	R5 075 675

TOTAL: R697 604 796

Tendai (Beast) Mtawarira, Danie Rossouw, Victor Matfield and Jannie du Plessis practise line-outs at Taupo, New Zealand, during the 2011 Rugby World Cup.

Willem Alberts and Fourie du Preez sign autographs at Taupo after training.

Training at Taupo, in preparation for the 30 September pool game against Samoa: from left to right, Beast, Heinrich Brüssow, Bismarck du Plessis, conditioning coach Derik Coetzee (partly hidden), Schalk Burger and Jannie du Plessis (26 September 2011).

Schalk Burger and fans at Taupo.

Coetzee. Meyer had an excellent record at the Blue Bulls and had nurtured the Bulls' contingent then dominating the Boks from the beginning of their careers. But there was a feeling that it was high time South Africa had a Springbok coach of colour. Coetzee would seem to have been the perfect candidate. He had been backline coach under Jake White when the Boks won the 2007 World Cup, so he could have contributed institutional memory to the coaching and management of the national team. Like De Villiers, Coetzee carried the scars inflicted by decades of apartheid's systemic dehumanisation. In this way, both speak to black South Africans who were brought up in the bad old days. Unlike De Villiers, Coetzee came through it without a chip on his shoulder and is a mature and socially skilled individual. I got to know Coetzee quite well while researching my last book, and he struck me as someone whom adversity had only strengthened. In 2012, the year he finally got to hold the reins, Western Province had its best year in a decade. In Super Rugby, he – and captain Jean de Villiers – led the Stormers to the top of the South African conference. They won the Currie Cup for the first time in eleven years, as well as the Vodacom Cup under coach John Dobson. I think Coetzee was the obvious choice for Springbok coach in 2008. But, unlike Peter de Villiers, he didn't have an ally in SARU's midst.

In his autobiography, *Politically Incorrect*, De Villiers writes about his relationship with Cheeky Watson, president of the Eastern Province union. He traces Watson's support for his candidacy to a declaration he had made to a journalist that Watson's son, Luke, could be Springbok captain. In another newspaper report, he was quoted as saying there were 60 black players who could be Springboks. De Villiers believes both statements played into Watson's twin political and personal agendas: to promote black players and to get his son into a Springbok jersey, preferably as captain.

De Villiers says that once it became clear to Cheeky Watson that he wasn't prepared to let the Eastern Province president influence his selections – including getting John Smit back from France to reassume the captaincy – Watson turned on him.

It's common cause now that Peter de Villiers largely let his senior players run the show. Whether he was the best candidate to succeed Jake White, or not, it is conceivable that he could have grown into the job had he not been fatally undermined by SARU's Teflon-coated president, who effectively said they'd appointed a quota coach, not the best coach. This fed every negative stereotype doing the rounds in South African rugby. The appointment of the first black coach, which should have been a visionary step forward, was, from the start, condemned as a disaster.

This, combined with the fact that he had inherited a World Cup-winning team, full of confidence, led to De Villiers relying increasingly heavily on the judgement of the more confident and experienced among them.

In his autobiography, Victor Matfield is clear about the extent of his own power. He relates in *My Journey* how, during a particularly fractious meeting between coaches and senior players during the Boks 2010 end-of-year tour, 'I got up, walked to the front and said: "We have to decide now what we must do and how we are going to play. The past three seasons we've been playing direct rugby from good field positions. If it seems like a good option to play the ball wide, then we'll do it, even in our own 22-metre area. But we never take unnecessary chances. We do not play high-risk rugby. That is how we, the Springboks, play."

'As nobody disagreed with me, we finally managed to reach consensus: we don't play like the All Blacks. We don't play like the Wallabies. We play Springbok rugby ...'

Later, he talks of why he valued Peter de Villiers: '... he had unfaltering faith in us and listened to what we had to say. And when things went wrong he often took up the cudgels for the team on even the smallest of issues ...'

I thought, reading this passage, of another incident at Taupo. I was, as usual in the evening when there was little else to do, sitting in the bar with the SuperSport guys, when Peter de Villiers again dropped by. Some bar owner in Wellington, he told us, was trying to claim that Victor had got up onto a counter and dropped his pants. What non-sense, he exclaimed. You know how tall Victor is – how could he possible stand up on a bar, he said, pointing to the one in front of us, which indeed did leave only a metre or so between the counter and the ceiling, nowhere near space enough for Victor's 2m frame. Nevertheless, I had heard elsewhere that this alleged incident was the cause of some stress. It probably explained why Victor looked so miserable throughout the World Cup.

England prop Mike Tindall was lambasted in the media for another bar incident – drunkenly embracing a woman who was not his royal wife – and his whole team and its campaign was affected by the fallout, much to the glee of the opposition. This was war. And any incident of misbehaviour, no matter how trivial, could be used by rivals.

Matfield also talks about how he and Peter 'discussed team selections'. It's no surprise, then, that the tenure of the first black coach was merely a change in the colour of the front guy. His assistant coaches were all white, as was the group of senior players upon whose judgement he relied so heavily. He had no effect whatever on the power of the dominant grouping in the Boks – the Bulls, led by Victor and Fourie du Preez – especially towards the end, when John Smit became so demoralised by the repeated calls for him to step down.

One could even argue that transformation within the team was set back by De Villiers's appointment. For instance, if De Villiers had not relied so heavily on Smit, selecting him perhaps when he should not have, the third-choice hooker, Chiliboy Ralepelle, might have had more opportunity. All this would have been forgotten, of course, if we had won. Matfield, Smit and De Villiers would all have been vindicated.

Throughout that New Zealand campaign, the tension between Jurie Roux and De Villiers was palpable. This fractious relationship between management and coach was one Roux inherited. He became CEO only late in 2010, so he was not involved in the appointment of De Villiers.

In fact, everything I have seen of his performance seems to indicate great efficiency. Individual tensions notwith-standing, everyone on the Bok management team in New Zealand appeared competent, hard-working and committed. The closer you get to the national team, the more effective the management. I don't think this is a coincidence. Accountability is the key. The performance of the Springboks and their coaches could not be more transparent: it's out there on the field for everyone to see. And to judge. They either win or lose. And they stand or fall on the result. The higher up you go, the more shadowy it becomes. The SARU General Council are accountable to no one but themselves. Several of them were in New Zealand, with their wives, courtesy of SARU. And they didn't fly cattle class.

As it turned out, Peter was given one extra month – January 2012 – as SARU dithered over who his replacement should be. Now he is out of the public eye, coaching the University of the Western Cape's rugby team, condemned to the near-obscurity he had feared.

The appointment of the Springbok coach and his subsequent management are the most high-profile of SARU's duties. Watching Peter at close quarters and Heyneke Meyer at some remove, I feel only sympathy for them. It seems to me that they are scapegoats, set up to fail. And this is a historical problem.

Rob van der Valk, who managed the Springbok team when Nick Mallett was head coach, wrote, with Andy Colquhoun, then a rugby writer, a memoir of his experience. In a better-run organisation, Mallett would have been fêted: his win rate, the only real calculator of performance, was 71%. This is higher than any other Springbok coach has achieved since and second highest since 1992, when the Springboks re-entered the international game. Mallett had a run of 17 consecutive Test wins, presiding over a total of 38. Only Kitch Christie tops his record, although with a much lower total: he won all 12 tests he was responsible for.

But Mallett didn't play politics. He didn't try to cultivate any allies in the SARU hierarchy. He just focused on one goal: winning games. Eventually, his bosses found a pretext to get rid of him when he was quoted as saying that ticket prices for Test games were too high. An eminently reasonable statement, one would have thought. But his contract stipulated that he was not allowed to criticise SARU publicly. His defence was that the woman to whom he had made the statement in response to a question had not identified herself as a journalist, so he was unaware that his comments would become public. Nevertheless, he was forced into an early exit from his job. SARU had to pay him out for the remainder of his contract. As they presumably had to do with Mallett's predecessor, Carel du Plessis. Neither of his successors, Rudolf Straeuli and Harry Viljoen, served their full terms.

The first coach to last the full four years between World Cups was Jake White, and his autobiography, too, records endless, grinding battles with his bosses.

What becomes clear when looking at the record of coaches over the past twenty-one years (see table on opposite page) is that they are viewed as expendable. In an organisation that relies on self-interest, mutual favours and secret deals, there is nothing to be gained from making an ally of a coach. He is there for only four years, if he's lucky. His job is to carry the can and then disappear.

Usually, when a coach is winning, he has a fair amount of immunity. As Peter de Villiers showed in 2009, when he won both the British and Irish Lions series and the Tri Nations. But, as soon as a coach starts losing – and, as records show, this is a third of the time, and 60% of the time in the

Springbok coaches' records since 1992

COACH (1st to last)	TESTS	WINS	WIN %	
John Williams (8/1992-11/1992)	5	1	20.00%	
Ian McIntosh (6/1993-8/1994)	12	4	33.335%	
Kitch Christie (10/1994-11/1995)	14	14	100%	
Andre Markgraaff (7/1996-12/1996)	13	8	61.54%	
Carel du Plessis (6/1997-8/1997)	8	3	37.50%	
Nick Mallett (11/1997-8/2000)	38	27	71.05%	
Harry Viljoen (11/2000-12/01)	15	8	53.33%	
Rudolph Straeuli (6/2002-11/2003)	23	12	52.71%	
Jake White (6/2004-12/2007)	54	36	66.67%	
Peter de Villiers (6/2008-10/2011)	48	30	62.5%	
Heyneke Meyer (6/2012-)	12	7	58.33%	

Tri Nations and its successor, the Rugby Championships – he becomes fair game.

Depressingly, the issues that have beset each Springbok coach for the past two decades have remained much the same. Which, one would have thought, proves that it is not the coach who is to blame, but the system itself.

The first issue is transformation: the proportion of players of colour in any Springbok squad. There is an element of cynicism here. Those who should be held responsible – those SARU unions that are failing in their duty to develop the game at the grass roots – can harangue successive Bok coaches sitting before them in performance appraisal meetings for not including (black) x, rather than (white) y. Making it personal and reductive exacerbates the fallout; it is hurtful and undermining for both black and white players, divisive for a team and piles unnecessary stress onto coaches. It also inflames the same old unproductive and unpleasant public debate, with one side complaining about black players being given unfair advantage and the other side branding all of rugby as racist.

The second perennial issue of contention is that of player contracts. Head coaches fight hard to get ultimate control over selection enshrined in their contracts because they rightly claim that, if they are to be held accountable for results, they need to be able to select the team. They achieve this but then find it subtly undermined by the allocation of player contracts. This process is always a protracted bunfight and becomes expensive for both sides, as senior counsel are employed. A great waste of money, one would have thought, which could have been far better used for better salaries for players and coaches or for development.

Following the 2011 World Cup, the year started with a raft of senior players having left the field and the arrival of several uncapped youngsters. For most of 2012, all the Boks, including captain Jean de Villiers and the Du Plessis brothers, the anchors of the team, were playing without contracts and therefore without pay or injury insurance, because they could not come to terms with SARU. This also meant that time and emotional energy that should have been employed on the game was spent fighting bosses instead. It was only towards the end of the year that the issue was resolved and they were finally paid.

In January 2013, the whole wearying process began again, and it wasn't until 24 April that 15 Boks were confirmed by SARU as being contracted. In the meantime, several of the country's finest players had announced their intention to leave for France, Japan and Ireland.

What head coaches want is the system under which New Zealand rugby operates: players are centrally contracted by the New Zealand Rugby Union and allocated to provincial teams. This means that the national team gets first call on players and that they are managed primarily for the benefit of the national team, rather than that of their union. So Richie McCaw can be given six months off in 2013 to rest in preparation for the run-up to the 2015 Rugby World Cup. Our national captain, by comparison, is played into the ground.

The New Zealand Rugby Union recognises the gem they have in Richie McCaw: at 33, he is still playing great rugby and has built up invaluable international experience. We have the same qualities – and a year less on the clock – in our captain, Jean de Villiers, but we apply the same wasteful short-termism to our players as we do to our coaches.

Western Province is Jean de Villiers's primary employer, and their interests supersede those of the Springboks. Understandably, there is no way they would give Jean de Villiers six months off from Super Rugby. The provincialism of South African rugby – the fact that individual unions put their interests above those of the national team – has another consequence. At the peak of their careers, players are heading off overseas, increasingly to Japan, where they are required to play fewer than 13 or 14 games a year and they can earn close to R1 million per game. Going overseas means not only that they build up savings for when their playing days are over, but also that they extend their careers. Their bodies are spared the punishing annual South African regimen of Super Rugby and Currie Cup, as well as Springbok Tests. In 2012, Jannie de Plessis, for example, played a total of 36 games: that is an average of three a month.

Heyneke Meyer watches impotently as the players he might have relied upon – Fourie du Preez, Jaque Fourie, JP Pietersen and Andries Bekker – say 'sayonara' as they disappear off to the Land of the Rising Sun.

The national coach gets access to his players for only four months of the year, and that is in the latter half of the year, when they are already feeling the effects of several months of Super Rugby. Their bodies have taken a battering and injuries are piling up. He has no control over how much rugby they play or how they are conditioned. Come the start of the international season in June, he must take what he can get.

Peter de Villiers has said that he learnt from his tenure as Springbok coach that one of the most daunting tasks was dealing with the media. It has to be said that De Villiers, the showman, courted some of this attention. Heyneke Meyer has been more successful in staying beneath the radar. Nevertheless, I think he too was shocked by the level of public vitriol directed at him during the away leg of the 2012 Rugby Championship. The coach I saw on his return from Australasia, before the first of the home games against the Wallabies at Loftus, was a different one from the relaxed, optimistic man I had had coffee with in February. The honeymoon was well and truly over. He had experienced the full fury of the media and the public over any number of issues: his continued support of Morné Steyn; his selection of Bulls players and his conservative game plan – and he was tense and angry.

In Springbok rugby, the coach bears the brunt of public scrutiny, facilitated by the media. His bosses – the union presidents – remain largely invisible. They never take the flak.

I found it fascinating to watch how Peter de Villiers was crucified by large parts of the media – and in the comments following online media reports – when he was appointed Springbok coach in 2008 because he wasn't Heyneke Meyer. Within a year of Meyer's assuming the position, he was being crucified – for being Heyneke Meyer and playing the game the way he has always played it: defence-based with lots of kick and chase. This was hardly a secret; it was the game he instituted at the Bulls and which the Bulls in the Springbok team reinforced.

It is clearly not good for South African rugby that Springbok coaches are treated in such a short-sighted way. Each of them builds up expertise and institutional knowledge that the country sorely needs. Each time, that experience and knowledge is thrown out when the next coach gains the hot seat for another short, fraught four years. Mallett, now back in the country and a commentator for SuperSport, was lost to France and then Italy for a decade. Surely we could be using him better than that? Jake White went to Australia, where he uses his South African experience to boost the Brumbies. Peter de Villiers at least has remained in the country, though one could argue that there are far more pressing causes requiring his expertise – such as in the Eastern Cape. But SARU wouldn't have him. Or Mallett, or White.

New Zealand, again, are far better at this. Graham Henry was head coach of the All Blacks for eight years and he was succeeded by one of his assistant coaches, Steven Hansen. Thus one of our main competitors builds intellectual capital, rather than wasting it, as South Africa does. We don't even keep assistants. They leave with the head coach and a whole new team must start from scratch, reinventing the wheel.

6 Logistics

I arrived in New Zealand on 3 September 2011, the day after the Boks did, and I booked into the same hotel, the five-star InterContinental in Wellington. As the incumbent world champions, they had first pick of accommodation. Some of the other competing teams had already arrived in New Zealand; the rest arrived shortly after we did. It felt like the invasion of a series of benign armies. The national teams bivouacking in towns and cities across these two small islands are so large – in numbers and in size – and so overwhelmingly male. And uniformly dressed, in their bright, solid team colours. Their numbers are multiplied by the camp followers: we, the media, with our obligatory accreditation cards swinging from our chests, and the fans, instantly identifiable in their team jackets, caps and scarves.

The logistics involved in shifting these armies around require military precision, as became clear to me from talking to Charles Wessels, the Springboks' logistics manager. Charles, I conclude after talking to him for an hour, could easily run a large corporation, such is his eye for both the detail of an operation and its overall picture. Over a cappuccino for me and a flat white for him, I get a sense of the enormous amount of planning and organisation that goes into a tour such as the World Cup.

Wessels himself is an unassuming man. He has a perpetually harassed expression and a light beard that looks more like a day or two of not having had time for even a shave.

Rugby got a grip on him early on, but at a time when black people's role in the game was heavily circumscribed. Born in 1961, he grew up in Grahamstown, where he attended the Mary Waters High School. 'There was only one sport – rugby. And, if you were selected for the first rugby team, you were made. Particularly among the opposite sex.'

After school, he spent three years at the University of the Western Cape (UWC), completing a BA degree in History and Sociology, and then returned to Grahamstown to do a degree in Higher Education at Rhodes. This was the politically turbulent 1980s, and Charles was deeply into anti-apartheid politics. For almost a year he was detained without trial by the security police.

'After liberation, I got onto the ANC proportional list and became deputy mayor of Grahamstown.' His CV, which he gives me later after much nagging, reveals a man whose life has been committed to public service. He has taught in public schools and occupied senior positions in the Eastern Cape government. He has coedited a book on political exiles and served on opera, library and university boards.

Rugby, though, has remained a passion. In 2004, he did a stint as Springbok logistics manager for Jake White. When De Villiers became coach, he was again asked to apply. At the time, he was on temporary secondment from his job as a senior manager in the office of the Secretary of the Eastern Cape legislature. One daughter had just graduated as a doctor and the second was studying to be one. 'They put pressure on me to fulfil my dream.' So he went ahead and applied, and has now been doing the job for three years.

He works from home in Port Elizabeth. Seven months a

year are spent at home and the other five on tour. 'Those seven months at home are the most important because that is when you plan and organise everything for the tours. I'm constantly on the phone and on email at two in the morning because that is when the Sanzar [South Africa, New Zealand and Australia Rugby] countries are awake.'

His planning for the World Cup began at the end of the Boks' New Zealand leg of their triumphant 2009 Tri Nations tour. Charles remained in New Zealand to do a reconnaissance of potential Bok bases for the World Cup. 'I stayed for seven days after we won the Tri Nations in Hamilton, so it saved SA Rugby a flight. They knew by then what the Boks' World Cup itinerary would be, at least for the first four weeks of the pool games.

'In Wellington and Auckland, I looked at hotels and at training grounds within twenty minutes' drive, as well a gym nearby. I motivated for those I thought the best and bounced it off senior players, who gave it the thumbs up.' Every detail of the tour is pored over.

'I look at things like our Energade supplier. And water. Water is problematic, in that it is expensive in New Zealand – R25 for a 500ml bottle – so, to cut costs, I have exchange agreements with Australia and New Zealand. We supply the water they need when they are in South Africa and they do the same for us when we tour.'

At the same time, discussions are begun with Canterbury, the team's clothing supplier: 'What clothes we want; what style; what kind of cloth.' And with Samsonite, the luggage supplier, for what kind of luggage they want.

Charles had set in motion the move to New Zealand

long before the boys boarded their Qantas flight from Johannesburg on 1 September. On 25 August, he sent 189 pieces of equipment to Wellington, consisting of physio requirements, elastic bands and other fitness equipment. Two bags for each of the guys. He remembers each of them.

'A total of 4 182kg! Two hundred and sixty-six pieces in total. It was collected on the 25th by DHL and all delivered and cleared by Customs and ready to be delivered to the hotel. And not one was lost! That is when you feel the plan is falling into place. The guys appreciate this – not having to struggle with two bags and a laptop bag. They only have to travel with one piece.'

If the new coach renews his contract, he will start planning the Rugby Championships tour soon after we get home.

'I will look at the Sanzar fixtures programme for next year – put it in blocks of weeks and present it to the coach for approval. So, firstly, I look at hotels that are appropriate – visit them, look for an appropriate training facility. And then liaise with Qantas to organise flights – it is difficult to get blocks of 45 seats in business class. This is the kind of thing I do off-season. You have to do it thoroughly. As they step off the bus, they get their keys.'

For the record, this was the Springboks' match day schedule for Saturday, 17 September 2011:

08.00-10.00	Breakfast
09.30-10.30	Preparation of change rooms Wellington Regional Stadium

Logistics

13.15-13.30	Stretching
13.30-14.00	Pre-match meal
14.30-16.00	Strapping, physiotherapy room
15.45	Logistics depart to Wellington Regional Stadium
16.00-16.15	Top-up meal
16.15	Non-playing reserves and management take their seats on the bus

Attire to stadium: Match 22 and on-field support staff wear presentation tracksuit, green polyester golf shirt, navy rain jacket. Head coach, assistant coaches, non-playing reserves and other officials wear green blazer, black pants, black shoes, white shirt, black belt, black socks, Springbok tie, sleeveless green jersey or white jersey. Black coat optional.

16.20-16.27	Team talk for Match 22 and coaches at InterContinental
16.29	Bus departs to Wellington Regional Stadium
16.35	Bus arrives at Wellington Regional Stadium
16.36	Confirmation of team and submission of match team sheet
16.40-16.43	On-field flash interview with coach
16.45-16.48	Clothing and equipment check, match officials briefing and front row instructions
16.45-17.15	Additional strapping
17.15	Kickers out

17.20	Coin toss. Decision regarding kickoff or receive or running direction can be immediate or latest by 17.30
17.22-17.42	Warm-up drills
17.30	Radio check
17.45	Field of play to be cleared
17.45	Coaches to their box
17.45	Countdown to run-on
17.51:30	Springboks leave change rooms. Presentation tracksuit bottoms. Teams assemble at mouth of tunnel
17.52:45	Flag bearers lead teams out to field
17.54	South African national anthem
17.57:45	South African line-up on 10m line for cultural challenge
18.01:30-18.43	South Africa vs Fiji first half
18.43-18.55	Half-time
18.55-19.40	South Africa vs Fiji second half
19.40-19.45	On-field flash interview with captain for Sky TV
19.45-19.50	In-tunnel interview with captain for SuperSport
19.50-19.55	In-tunnel interview with head coach for Sky NZ and SuperSport
19.50-20.30	Recovery – individual 10-minute massages
19.58-20.05	In-tunnel interviews with at least four players for SuperSport and general rights holders
20.20-20.35	Post-match media conference with coach and captain

Logistics

21.00-21.20   Mixed zone for minimum 10 personnel,
                  including two coaches and captain
Springbok bus departs to InterContinental Hotel after
   conclusion of mixed zone
Players assemble in team room on arrival
Team meeting
Dinner

The day after the match against Fiji, when the team decamped to Taupo, on the North Island, the schedule for the move went like this:

All luggage to the team room by 04.50 on Sunday 18 September 2011
Only one carry-on wheelie bag of 7kg plus laptop bag will be allowed for carry-on
Blue jeans, white polyester golf shirt, lime retro jacket with green field jacket, shoes/cross-trainers and underwear must be kept by players

Sunday 18 September 2011

06.00   Collection of luggage and equipment to be transported to Taupo
06.00-07.00   Breakfast
07.05   Bus departs to Wellington International Airport

Blue jeans, white polyester golf shirt, lime retro jacket (green field jacket optional)

08.40   Depart to Taupo on chartered flight
09.40   Arrival at Taupo airport

10.00	Bus transfer to Bayview Wairakei Resort
11.30	Sandwiches, snacks and drinks
12.00	Bus departs for Opotaka
13.00-16.00	Marae visit and reception by Paramount Chief Tumu Te Heuheu
16.10	Bus depart to Bayview Wairakei Resort
18.30-18.55	Media conference with a coach
19.00	Prayer: Bryan Habana
	Dinner

Technical meeting with Peter, Rassie, Jacques, Dick, Malome, Neels, Derik, Percy

Since Heyneke Meyer's arrival, Charles has been put on the permanent staff and relocated to SARU's head office in Cape Town. His biggest job now is a detailed reconnaissance of the British cities, hotels, practice grounds and stadia from which the Boks will launch their campaign for the 2015 Rugby World Cup.

7 Maintenance

When Jean de Villiers tore his rib cartilage in the opening game of the World Cup in Wellington, he faced the devastating prospect of early ejection from his third World Cup. Until Dr Craig Roberts got to work on him.

Craig took blood from Jean de Villiers and used a centrifuge to concentrate the blood platelets. Then, using an ultrasound for maximum accuracy, he injected the platelets, suspended in plasma, directly into Jean's damaged cartilage in an attempt to speed up his recovery.

'Some feel these platelet-rich plasma injections are very useful and some don't,' he tells me. 'My feeling is that, in certain situations, they can be very useful, and we have managed to return guys to play 40% quicker, but only for certain specific things. What it works really well with is rib cartilage injuries like Jean's. By using the platelet-rich plasma injection, we will be able to get him back quite quickly. So, with cartilage injuries, it works well. Some muscle tears, it works well. You take the patients' own blood, spin it down and then you extract their platelets and then inject the platelets suspended in the plasma back into the injured areas. So it's the platelets that do the healing.'

I'm fascinated by this. Especially because all of it was done by Craig alone in his room at Wellington's InterContinental Hotel.

A Bok doc needs to be an all-rounder: versatile and self-sufficient. Craig Roberts is a one-man travelling ER show, putting together broken bodies and doing his bit for battered emotions as well. He brings everything he needs with him, courtesy of the logistical skills of colleague Charles Wessels: 'I've got a portable ultrasound. I've used it at half-time and after the game a lot. It has revolutionised things in that you can make a diagnosis in the change room and decide immediately how best to manage it. So I'll do one ultrasound right after the game and then another one on the Monday, which is probably more accurate because the bleeding has settled by then. Especially when you are overseas, you don't want to go out and get a scan done and then perhaps see another specialist and then delay the whole process. It's not as easy here [on tour in New Zealand] to get MRIs and things. And then, if you need to do injections, you can do it via ultrasound.'

Craig Roberts is a tall, lean man with an attractive, open face. He is based in Durban, where he is also the Sharks team doctor. With his fair, shaggy hair and relaxed manner, he looks more like a surfer than a rugby player.

But it is rugby that is his passion, he says, and it always has been. Now 42, he played loose forward at his school, the elite St Stithians College, in Johannesburg, and went on play for UCT while studying medicine there. After graduating, he went to the UK, where he practised orthopaedics, before returning to South Africa and registering for a master's degree in Sports Medicine at the Sports Science Institute in Cape Town.

'The reason I studied medicine was to be a rugby doctor,' he says. 'I didn't want to be stuck in an office dealing with snotty-nosed kids and grannies.'

In 2001, he did a year as Bok doc. 'And then, when Peter became coach, he asked me to be the Springbok doctor again. I love it, hey. I'm hoping to go on doing it.'

His wish has been granted. The entire Springbok medical team – Craig Roberts, physiotherapists Rene Naylor and Vivian Verwant, and massage therapist Daliah Hurwitz – have been given new four-year contracts under Heyneke Meyer.

It was clear to me during the World Cup that this was one of the more crucial units in the team. Game plans and selections you can control, but injuries you cannot. The Boks are continually poleaxed by injuries – and we will continue to be. Each game, injury is what we fear most. After loss, of course. Doc Roberts is the one who assesses and heals. Or who cannot. He strides up and down the side of the field during training and during games, ever-watchful for a strain or a blow. Ever-ready to rush to an injured player's side. The mobile A&E department. Back at the hotel, at all hours, he labours over battered bodies. It's frequently touch and go whether they're up to playing or not.

I put this to Craig: who makes the final decision as to whether, and when, a player is fit to play?

'My medical team and I will consult with the player and the coach. But the decision comes down to me. The decision whether a player is ready to be selected is quite an intricate thing, because a lot of players play with niggles. Especially after a long Super Rugby season and then the World Cup. They might have a stiff back or ankle that every now and again gets a bit swollen. But that's rugby, and a lot of guys just push through with that. A lot of people don't realise that the guys are playing with some sort of discomfort. The main thing I consider when deciding whether to put a guy on the field is whether it will make the injury worse. You don't want to put a guy on and then what was a ten-day injury becomes a six-month injury. And the other criterion is: can he perform on the field? If he can't make a tackle with his left shoulder and he's vulnerable in defence on that side, he will let himself and the team down.'

In the last few weeks before travelling to New Zealand, the players were being monitored on a weekly basis. 'We had a cut-off point: the guys have to be fit by a certain date in order to be eligible for the World Cup.'

Once in New Zealand, it's a case of careful management. 'You look at the longer term. You might have a guy who was injured and would be out for three weeks and we would be managing him through the pool games and hopefully be ready for the quarterfinals, the semifinals and hopefully the final. So you still are managing the guys with longer-term injuries. But it's literally week by week. Will he be ready in seven days, and in some cases, will he be ready in five days, for the game? And that is where experience counts: you know how players will respond. And sometimes you have to make late decisions. You have to do a fitness test and see whether a player is ready or not.'

What does a fitness test involve? 'There's no specific thing,' he responds. 'It depends on the injury and on the position of the player. There are certain demands on a wing, for instance. What a wing needs to do on the field is very different from what a prop needs to do on the field, so it really involves a functional assessment based on the stresses he would be subjected to in a game. It might be a shoulder. It might be a hamstring. So we would put him through scenarios that would replicate what he might have to do, and see how he responds, and, based on that, you can make an assessment of whether he might be fit for the game or not.

'There are some players who have incredibly high pain thresholds and can push through things. Schalk is one. Butch James is another one – if you look at his knees and how well he's done with that. He plays with discomfort and he manages it. But every player is different. There are different demands. What counts for me is whether putting a guy on the field will make it worse. I think there are times when players try to keep things from the medical staff because they want to get back on the field, but we can pick it up in training. We can see when a guy is struggling or worried about something. And I think, in the professional era, guys are becoming more responsible about that. They don't want to let the team down, and if they go on with an injury they will do just that. And it comes down to trust. If the players trust us and trust our judgement, they will listen to us. The guys know I'm not going to pull them for any little thing. It's not a cut-and-dried thing: there are lots of nuances.

'If they play on a Saturday, say, we assess all the players in the change room and get an idea which guy has problems. Sunday is usually a rest day, although some of the guys with problems get treatment. By the Monday morning management meeting, you've got a relatively good indication of the severity of the injuries, and then you can make a call about when they will be ready and when not. It's very easy just to rule a guy out, but I try to give a guy as much opportunity as possible. It's tough for them.'

The physios and the conditioning team help to keep players fit. 'We screen each player to identify which areas are at risk, so we try to prevent injuries before they happen. They get specific exercise programmes or rehab based on that. Once you are into the World Cup, a lot of it is managing the guys through that: enhancing their recovery and making sure they are ready for the next game. So your prevention stuff has to be done before the tournament, because you don't want to have to do too much during the campaign.'

I ask him about the little GPS monitor tucked into a pocket on the back of each player's jersey. It's a question he likes because the Boks made history here. 'We were the first team to get permission from the IRB to wear GPSs during Test matches. It was a voluntary thing: we didn't force the guys to do it. But most wore it during training and during games. It gives a good idea of the distance travelled – the speed at which they travelled – and it's got an accelerometer built into it that gives an indication of collision and force of collisions, so you can measure the actual body load on the players.

'It's a very nice tool because we can monitor the load of training and also the load of each player in the game. On a Sunday after a game, we can look at the data to see which player has worked really hard, because it gives their heart rate as well as distance, velocity and impact. So it's a very useful tool for managing the actual load of the players. Because in rugby it's very different for different players, and the load on each is different. We've been doing it for two years working up to the World Cup because you need a baseline to see what's normal.'

Heart rate throughout the game is recorded, as is any

impact – whether a tackle, a scrum, hitting a breakdown or coming down from a line-out. 'We get an indication of what those forces are for all players.'

This information is available in real time to him on the edge of the field, so he can follow what is happening to a player, but usually he downloads it after a game and then analyses it.

'Literally an hour after a game, we can have all the info downloaded onto a computer. It's useful for training as well: we know which guys have had a really heavy game and we didn't want them doing too much on the Monday and Tuesday. We want to optimise their recovery. So, if their training volumes start getting a bit high, we would watch it live and then pull them out of training once they reach a certain level. And then, if a guy's got a little bit of flu or a snotty nose and is still able to train, I can watch his heart rate during the session.'

All this information is presented to a management meeting on the day after the game. 'We go though the game and go through all that data.'

He carries around his own medical supplies. 'You've got to anticipate what might happen. I bring back the vast majority of what I take, but you have to expect the worst. I travel with a lot of emergency equipment, like defibrillators. There are incidences of collapse and sudden death on the field. You do screen the guys in advance, but you can't screen for everything.'

The arrival of union presidents and their wives, most of them elderly, for the quarterfinals adds to Craig's workload, although he does not complain. What probably adds to his value is the fact that he is a team player. His commitment is unselfish and wholehearted. Even the travelling band of South African media calls on his services. 'I've probably got 100 people dependent on me. It's difficult to see a doctor in a foreign place, so, if I can help them, I will. I've have had journos knocking on my door at three in the morning.'

It's a hectic schedule. 'From 7am, we go flat out till 10 at night. There is the morning training session, the afternoon gym session; in between are medical sessions and management sessions, and then we will try to get a session with the players in between. I might see 20 players in a day, but the physios really work very hard: they might go on till 10 or 11 at night to get everyone done.'

Craig goes to all the management meetings because it helps him to get a sense of the demands on the players, and vice versa. But also because he is in a position to get messages from coaches to players on the field, so he needs to be alert to the game plan.

'Being on the side of the field, I'm a conduit, so I must know what's been planned for that week – what calls are being made, and so on. Because, although your primary role is to take care of the players, it's also very much about communication. There are rules about when you can go on the field. If a player is injured, we can go on the field and deal with the injury, but when you are on the field you can get a lot of messages through. Some of the coaches give a lot of messages. Others don't. And then we can also give messages from the edge of the field, too. We are allowed to roam up and down the touchline and I do give a lot of messages from the side of the field all the time.'

Peter de Villiers did not want a sports psychologist on his team, even though the players had requested one. It appeared to me to be an egotistical decision. De Villiers explains in his autobiography that he wanted the players to confide in him. He saw a psychologist as a rival to this intimacy. He seemed to have failed to understand that his power over the players meant he could not provide the impartial and confidential services of a professional. As a result, Craig had to help fill that role, too.

'A lot of my job is sports psychology. Different players react differently to injury. It's about trying to ensure a player is in the right frame of mind when he goes back onto the field, and also if he's not going to go back on the field. I also see my role as injecting positivity. To me, you are either a person who gives energy or you take energy away. I see my role as always to be consistent and positive. You are not up and down.

'When a guy is down, you try to pick him up. Give him the right feedback at the right time. The medical staff is very much a conduit between the coaching staff and the players.

'The coaches don't have a lot of direct contact with the players. They speak to them, but there's not a lot of one-on-one, whereas the medical team, and particularly the physios, have them to themselves for half an hour, so there is a window of opportunity there to gain their trust and to work on them as well. It comes with time. Everyone's different, and you have to learn the different nuances. For example, if Schalk complains that something is sore, I know it's very sore. Another player might complain and we know it's not that bad and we can push him. But that comes with time.

You've got to develop a relationship with players and a kind of respect that comes with that.

'You need to be acutely aware when a player is dropped, when a player is down and why he's down. And sometimes it is unrelated to rugby. You've got to remember the guy is away from home. Some get homesick. They miss their kids. They miss their wives. The coach's big role is to keep the seven players on the bench happy and the five or six who didn't make the 22 happy. The guys who are starting are fine. It's not always easy.

'It's tough for the players. I don't think the public realises that they almost get trapped in their rooms, because every time they come downstairs there are fifty people wanting autographs, and the public get upset when they don't do the autographs. They do become a bit claustrophobic. But, having said that, as a management team, you can get around that. We have outings with the team. And Wednesday is traditionally a day off. So a lot of guys will go and play golf and get out into the fresh air. It's a ritual for a lot of the guys. It's part of their preparation for the Test. If we tried to stop that, there'd be a revolt. But I think it's a good thing. You need to switch off mentally from the stresses of the rugby environment, and Wednesday is a good day to do it.

'You do need to be able to switch on and off as a player. You can't have rugby consuming you all the time. Southern hemisphere teams are used to long tours – five weeks is the norm. Northern hemisphere teams don't have that – Heineken Cup tours are only two days. And long tours are good for team-building: the old school rugby *gees*.'

But, as in every other respect, the national team comes second to the demands of the provincial unions. And suffers for it. 'We were peaking at the right time. The whole campaign had been carefully managed. There was a long tapering-off period after Super Rugby because it was such a long season – the first time they had done it. And the way they did that was, at their franchises, they really had to cut down on their training. So we got the players going into the World Cup not at the level we normally would, which is understandable after such a long competition. We knew we would be going into the World Cup a little bit undercooked.'

* * *

Rene Naylor lives in an apartment in the posh Mandela Rhodes Place in central Cape Town. She also has consulting rooms in the luxurious spa on the ground floor where I have arranged to meet her. As she comes towards me, I notice what a striking woman she is. In New Zealand, her glamour was so often hidden by the shapeless Springbok tracksuits. Now she wears a navy-blue wraparound dress, which shows off her figure. She is very slim but discreetly muscled. Small as she is, I can see how she manages to get a grip on those large rugby players. Long black hair swings around her face. Her high heels click commandingly on the tile floor.

Feminine but formidable, she strikes me as a very sexy woman. Now in her late thirties, she's carved out an exciting, unorthodox life in a highly competitive, male-dominated field. She's seized her opportunities as they came up, made the most of them, and then created new ones for herself.

Like Peter de Villiers, Rene comes from a Cape coloured

family, and, like him, I imagine she hasn't always had it easy. She tells me that she grew up watching rugby in Belhar on the Cape Flats. She went to school there and then studied Physiotherapy at UWC. After that came a postgraduate degree in Sports Physiotherapy at the Sports Science Institute in Cape Town. Her research was in rugby. 'Because I'd grown up with rugby, when my first rugby player came to me for treatment and said, "Why don't you come and help us?", I did.' This was at the Silvertree Rugby Club, in Mitchells Plain. She went on to establish her own physiotherapy practice in Mitchells Plain. It has now grown to accommodate two psychologists and a psychiatrist as well.

Her first foray into treating professional players was with the Western Province Under-19s. At the time, this batch included Schalk Burger and Andries Bekker, so she knows them pretty well. She moved up with them to treat the Under-21s. Then the first team and the Stormers. And, finally, she got to be Bok physio.

Two years ago, she moved to Mandela Rhodes Place. When she is home, she treats mostly recreational athletes at the spa. At the moment, one of the physios at her Mitchells Plain practice is off sick, so, for the first time in eight years, she is working there too.

I ask her to describe what it was like to be part of the management team at the World Cup. Every day is different, she says. 'I think that, when I wake up, I will do my own training and then do the strapping. But then a guy comes in and says he has cramps, and the coach says he wants to know today about a player's condition. So you have to be both very flexible and very structured.'

On match days, she starts strapping four hours before kickoff. 'Guys like routine on a match day. Everyone gets five minutes per joint. The tape is pre-cut. The purpose of strapping is, firstly, to protect an old injury – you use rigid tape for that. Coloured tape is used either to protect a muscle or to make it contract and work better.

'You can only do six or seven guys at the field. I try to give the senior players preference. But all the guys who are starting get preference. Some want to have showers first and shave their legs.'

At half-time, she and Craig Roberts check for injuries. 'The coach gives us the first two minutes at half-time. We will go through the squad. Craig goes through the forwards. I do the backs. We are very unobtrusive, so, if the coach wants to talk, he can do that. If they need ice, we give it to them. If they're injured and still want to play, you assess it. If they've had a knock, I inform the doc and he tells the coach: "Just watch this guy." But, if you are dealing with elite players, they've got good body awareness. They know if it's serious or not.

'Often with concussion, players believe they can continue playing. They might dispute your opinion because they are confused. But usually they trust us.'

In the change room immediately after a game, she and Craig again check every player for new injuries. They then begin their recovery protocol: 'Every player who has played more than 40 minutes has a ten-minute rubdown on any area that is sore. They wear compression garments and we put them on an electronic ice machine. If we are concerned about a swelling, he sleeps with it on – it's programmed to go on and off for 30 minutes all night. Ice is the primary post-injury treatment, and the electronic ice machine is a thousand times more effective than an ice pack because that gets to body temperature in a few minutes.'

A call often needs to be made at this point about whether an injury will need further investigation. Or the player might feel fine at the time but might wake up sore.

The IRB appoints a medical officer in each town where a World Cup team is based. The medical officer will organise any care the visitors' medical team can't give. Scans that Craig and Rene feel need expert scrutiny are sent back to their preferred specialists in South Africa.

Rene, like Craig, carries around an arsenal of equipment. 'You have to have enough stock for each guy for the whole of the World Cup. You know by now what each guy needs: 23kg of tape per week – 10kg per match. I also carry 23kg of braces – ankle guards, slings, back braces – for every joint and every size for every joint. So, if a player needs crutches or braces, I have them ready.'

By September 2011, the medical team has been together for four years, and has evolved a seamlessly efficient operation. Especially for match days, when the players are so hyped up that any deviation in routine is upsetting. 'Everyone knows what everyone else is doing. When you get to the change room, it is all calm and well organised. The last thing you want is that someone is late and a guy is worrying he will be late for the warm-up.'

She has developed an academic speciality in injury prevention and is working towards a PhD. 'I started in 2006 with Janine Grey, who works in cricket. We decided we needed a tool to assess players to see where they are at risk. We spent two years developing a [software] tool. Most tests are for lower limbs and shoulders, for both cricket and rugby. In 2008, we tested it on the Springboks.'

Each player now has his own risk profile, available in handy colour codes. 'I can tell if this one is at high risk for hamstring injury, say. So that area will show red for high risk.

'Say this is Jean de Villiers: all his past injuries would be highlighted, and we would know his calves are at high risk for injury. In 2010, I took it a step further. It was clear that the tool was working well in that it does predict injuries, so now we have to show which exercises will strengthen their vulnerable parts.'

Because players spend so much of their time at their franchises, she tests them there as well, not just when they join the Boks, so that their care over the year is consistent.

There are some universal predictors of injury. Once you are over twenty-three, the risk of muscle strain increases – the older you are, the bigger the risk of strain. But the most reliable predictor of injury is previous injury, and here the two meet. 'Older guys have played more rugby and have had more injuries, and their healing mechanisms are not as great as those of a young player.'

The intensive treatment players get on tour helps: 'I see the guy all day – I can make sure he lies down the first two days, uses his crutches and comes to me for treatment often. You can make sure he is eating and sleeping properly.'

Every morning, the injured player's wellbeing is monitored. 'Injury affects a player so much – you can see if a guy is injured. He is low, he is down, he is not sleeping well. So that is why there is close attention to a player who is not necessarily asking for it. You say: "Please let me assess that niggle."

'We've moved away from the "let's be tough" macho system. They must report it if they're very stiff or sore or "Gosh, this hamstring is tight!" Obviously there must be a balance. You mustn't wrap them in cotton wool, and you can't allow a guy to abuse the system by using niggles to get out of training, for instance. You have to assess it properly and see that if it is legitimate.'

I ask her what it's like being female in such a testosterone-heavy environment, and particularly in the physically intimate area of injury and treatment. She replies tartly: 'I suspect it would be more pertinent to ask the players!' And then she goes on: 'I don't expect anything different because I'm female – I expect to be respected as a professional. I certainly don't feel it strange to walk into a change room and I don't think they've treated me differently. I'd like them to see me first as a professional before they see me as a woman. But you must be able to take a joke as well, and I don't want the guys to behave differently around me.'

From what I've seen of Rene Naylor, she is perfectly capable of determining how she is treated. I admire her steel, not only in achieving what she has, but also in hanging onto it. There are loads of young physios who would kill to do her job for free, she says. But she's not giving it up any time soon.

* * *

A top Springbok needs to be equipped not only with a strong work ethic, athletic genes and an appetite for risk; he also needs to have a good brain and a high level of emotional intelligence.

Professor Tim Noakes from the Sports Science Institute in Cape Town is unequivocal about this. 'The very best athletes have to be both very clever and very emotionally astute,' he says. They need aggression but it has to be carefully calibrated. Use it to dominate an opponent, but keep it within the ever-changing rules or you will let your team down by attracting penalties and yellow and red cards. A Springbok player has to deal with the fact that every time he sets foot on the field he risks a career-ending injury. He has to come to terms with this threat and then conquer the concomitant emotion: fear.

Rugby players are risk-takers. Every time they run onto the field, they take a risk – primarily of injury but also of failure and rejection. So many boys dream of making it into the green and gold jersey. So few do. Yet they go on putting their all into it. This also speaks to a strong addictive element.

Two sports science researchers, named, confusingly, Matthew Pain and Matt Pain, from Loughborough University in the UK write in the leading British medical journal *The Lancet* that risk-takers have an evolutionary edge: 'Early man first came out of Africa about 100 000 years ago. Confronted by new and hazardous environments, our ancestors were forced to take great risks and travel large distances to find food, shelter and sexual partners. So-called risky genes were therefore adaptive and became more common through natural selection ...'

The Matthews Pain identify dopamine, the neurotransmitter associated with the pleasure system of the brain, as the reinforcer of risk-taking. 'It is released by naturally rewarding experiences such as eating and sex, and also survival behaviours like fighting and scavenging. Activities that are extremely engaging, intense and novel can also trigger the dopamine reaction. Thus the same mechanism that rewarded our ancestors for acting to stay alive may also underpin the highs afforded by extreme sports.'

But risk-takers are not necessarily reckless. On the contrary, the risks they take are carefully calculated. 'Extreme sports demand perpetual care, high degrees of training and preparation and, above all, discipline and control. Most of those involved are well aware of their strengths and limitations in the face of clear dangers.'

Peter de Villiers might not have wanted a counsellor on his team, but Heyneke Meyer does. He appreciates the significance of the psychological factor in performance. All players have off-field issues at some point or another, he says. All could use the services of a professional.

Being off-balance psychologically can have as much impact on a player's game as insufficient conditioning or skills training. Take, for example, the sudden and dramatic fall-off in the form of the normally reliable Morné Steyn in mid-2012. The Bulls and Springbok flyhalf is the second-highest scoring Springbok, bested only by Percy Montgomery. Then, suddenly, in 2012, he started fluffing kicks at goal, culminating in a 21-11 loss to the All Blacks in a game the Boks could have won had Steyn not missed four out of five kicks at goal.

Steyn's father, Johan, had been arrested for burglary shortly before his son's dramatic loss of form. His wife also gave birth to their first baby at this time. This sudden life change, plus the trauma of his father's fall from grace, seems to imply an automatic correlation with his inability to find the small space between the goalposts. Of all players, a flyhalf needs to be able to quickly find that deep, calm place within himself that will enable him to shut out everything around him and reduce the world to his boot, the ball and the exact trajectory it will need to follow to find that distant space between the goal posts.

In the 2011 Rugby World Cup, Morné Steyn had scored 62 points, to become the highest-scoring player in the World Cup, a feat rendered even more impressive by the fact that the Boks were ejected at the quarterfinals and therefore played only five games. I asked him how he managed to achieve that meditation-like stillness, especially in the case of a conversion, when it comes in the immediate aftermath of the rush and excitement of the try, at a time when the opposition fans will be at their most crushed and therefore most virulent.

It's all about practice, he says. In the week before a game, he has kicked 100 to 200 times. 'You take that to the field. You shut out the 50 000 or whatever people, you don't think about what will happen after the kick, what will be said. You shut out all negativity. You keep all that stuff out.'

Ironically, Steyn rediscovered his form as goal-kicker during the same game that saw the drop in form of another Springbok flyhalf, also for father-related reasons. In the first 2013 Super Rugby game between the Bulls and the Stormers, Elton Jantjies made his debut for the Stormers. A few weeks before, he had lost his 46-year-old father, who was also his manager, to a freak allergic reaction to a bee sting.

Usually, the issues are less dramatic but nevertheless distracting: a sick child, a fight with a girlfriend, money worries. Or, as with players from difficult backgrounds like Siya Kolisi, the burden of an extended family's welfare weighing you down.

That is why sound emotional grounding in the early years – such as that given to the Du Plessis brothers and to Jean de Villiers – is so important. It gives the player a rock-steady foundation on which to build. Jannie and Bismarck du Plessis bear out Noakes's theory of the integral part that sophisticated emotional intelligence plays in performance at the highest level. Without it, they would not have been able to manage the dual demands of studying while playing professionally and then, in Jannie's case, holding down a very demanding parallel job. Not to mention the ongoing stress of their father's painful decline.

Jannie has now taken on two extra roles – husband and father – and, initially at least, he struggled with these. After the Sharks' shock loss to the Brumbies in the 2013 Super Rugby campaign, coach John Plumtree actually benched his Springbok tighthead. The reason? Jannie was struggling with the demands of a heavily pregnant wife and imminent fatherhood on top of both day jobs.

Managing a family as a Springbok is not easy because of the incessant travel. But, for those who do it successfully, it provides a comfort zone. Jean de Villiers's mantra is: you need to surround yourself with 'good people'. He is referring to family and friends and, also, presumably, his agent. It interests me that, as usual with this free spirit, he has thought outside the box in his choice of agent. Stan Matthews is from the soccer world, which is largely black, reflecting an entirely different sector of society from that of rugby.

De Villiers's high level of emotional intelligence is evident in the quality of his leadership. Ian Schwartz, the Springbok manager, told me Jean was the best captain he had ever worked with. 'He is just such a brilliant role model.' One of De Villiers's strengths is his capacity to keep on coming back, constantly finding new resources to meet new challenges. Frequently, he has been written off as past his prime. Each time, he proves his critics wrong.

Sitting on a bench on the edge of the Stormers' training ground, De Villiers talks about the psychological complexities of managing a team. 'People just see the end result and there is a lot that you do that they don't see. There's a lot of work that goes on just to get the guys motivated week out and week in and to keep the guys in line, because there are so many different characters and personalities that you are working with,' he explains. 'So there has to be a difference in how you approach each guy and how you communicate with them.'

De Villiers is in favour of a team counsellor because he sees the effects of individual emotional imbalance. 'What happens in your personal life affects your team a lot. Even though you might not realise it, what you do has an effect on your fellow players and it's just making the guys realise that. Each and every guy has a responsibility toward the team, and, at the end of the day, if you do something wrong, it's the guy next to you that you are hurting. Once you get a team to play for each other, there is no way that you can lose. You will die for each other and do everything you can to be successful.'

De Villiers knows those subtle subterranean currents that swell beneath the game. When they are in full force, they create a magical fluidity. The Matthews Pain identify this as 'flow' – 'the freedom of complete absorption and suspension of time' – that is one of the most pleasurable sensations available to humans. A transcendence that invites addiction.

It is all emotion or *gees*: intangible, unteachable. It takes an intuitive, skilled leader to evoke it. De Villiers says that shifting the focus can do it, 'If you think that success is sometimes not what you win in trophies but the friends that you make,' thus strengthening the bonds – crucial in this ultimate of team sports. Or of defeating the odds – going in as underdogs and coming out on top: 'When you achieve something people don't think you can achieve, that can be success as well. And overcoming stumbling blocks.' Such as devastating injuries to key members of the team, like the torn cruciate ligament that felled Schalk Burger in the first Super Rugby game of 2012.

Some rugby coaches caution that players who become fathers tend to lose form. New babies mean less sleep. More fundamentally, these consummate risk-takers suddenly find themselves with a life-changing responsibility.

But, for De Villiers, it's only been a plus. 'When I think back now, I can see the change in how I approach things and how I work with my fellow players. It really has changed my life significantly. Just the responsibility in everything I do. I think I'm a better captain now than I was before I was a dad.'

8 The Wives and Girlfriends

The Bayview Wairakei Resort in Taupo has a small guest laundry: two washing machines and two dryers where you can do your own washing, for a nominal fee. During the World Cup, Taupo was where many of the Springbok wives and girlfriends arrived to join their men because there was a ten-day break between games. This, Peter de Villiers explained to me, was a delicate period: after three weeks and three wins, the guys are beginning to relax. This is when they might go off the rails. It was as well to have their women here to contain them.

The Springboks get their laundry seen to, but wives and girlfriends are on their own. As a result, this little room becomes a hothouse of domesticity. One evening, I am having a drink in the bar with the SuperSport guys, trying to remember when my washing cycle is due to finish and I must race upstairs and empty it, because there is high demand now. I arrive a little late and find the machine empty. I open one dryer – in case someone has kindly transferred my wet washing – and find it full of women's clothes, but not mine. Bryan Habana pads in; they are his wife's clothes. He's doing her laundry. I eventually discover my washing is in the other dryer. Then Juan de Jongh comes in, trailed by his and Gio Aplon's bubbly girlfriends. They tell me about their day – skiing on an artificial snow slope – while they stuff their washing into Habana's newly vacated dryer. Tomorrow night, they move to another five-star hotel, where this kind of self-sufficiency won't be offered, and where every service has to be handsomely paid for.

By no means all the wives and girlfriends have come to Taupo. And those who are there keep a low profile. I sometimes spot Johann Muller's blonde wife and little daughter walking through the garden to their outside room, on their way to the BP shop across the road or to the swimming pool. But I seldom see them in the main section of the hotel. From what I gather, some players' marital relations are strained. One was heard to mutter: 'As sy kom, dan gaan ek' ('If she comes, I'm going'). Another's wife phones frequently in floods of tears, which is not helpful to the morale of her husband on the other side of the world.

There tends to be an informal hierarchy among the wives, which tallies with their husbands' levels of seniority in the team. Many of the women are also professionals: John Smit's wife, Roxy, is an accountant; Victor Matfield's, Monja, is a dentist; Ronel du Plessis, Jannie's wife, is a doctor.

The Springbok staff member who takes care of the women is public relations officer AnneLee Murray. It is always an issue whether, and to what extent, women can accompany their husbands or boyfriends on tour. Former Ikey Tigers loose forward JJ Gagiano was part of the United States team at the World Cup. His girlfriend, Lisa Brown, followed him to New Zealand but had to book into a different hotel from the one the team was staying in. 'The wives and girlfriends had to creep around,' she recalled. 'Even on JJ's day off, if he wanted to meet me for lunch, he'd have to ask the coach, but he also didn't want to seem distracted.'

It is generally the head coach who sets the tone. AnneLee,

a highly competent, motherly woman who has been with the Boks for more than a decade, says that some Springbok coaches don't want the wives around. But, generally, coaches try to make it work for everyone. The players perform better if their families are happy, and AnneLee takes it upon herself to make sure they are.

'I book the wives' air tickets and arrange for them to get picked up from the airport. We have a suite for them so that they can breastfeed. I don't have to. But I also don't want the player to worry about anything but the task at hand. Because, if the wife is not happy, the player isn't happy.'

The wives of the captain and the other senior players tend to take charge of the others. 'Roxy Smit was a pillar of strength as the captain's wife. She would take the other women under her wing and tell them: this is what you do and what you don't do.'

She works closely with the captains: 'Andre Vos was my first captain. Then Joost van der Westhuizen. The captains I have been closest to are John Smit, Victor Matfield and Jean de Villiers. I have known Victor and John since they first became Springboks. I went to their weddings and I am John Smit's sons' godmother.'

During the fraught build-up to the game against the All Blacks in the 2012 Rugby Championship at Soccer City in Soweto, the wives gathered for a baby shower for Adriaan Strauss's wife – all organised by AnneLee.

I talk to AnneLee in SARU's new offices in Plattekloof. They have just moved here from Newlands and it still feels a bit strange, this modern concrete and glass building well away from the hubbub of the field. But the office in which I sit with AnneLee is bright and spacious. Light pours in through big windows.

She recalls with a smile the first time Schalk introduced Michele, now his wife, to his team-mates. 'It was in 2003. Schalk had played a few Tests but had never brought a girl along. Then he said to me: "I've met a nice girl and I want her to come to the Test. What must I do?" So, I said: "Well, tell her to come to the hotel and I will arrange it from there." And he said: "But she can't drive. She's still at school!"'

A fiftieth cap is a big deal for a player, and their families are brought in, either to the hotel or to the change room, for a champagne celebration. Some parents – Fourie du Preez's and Jean de Villiers's, for example – travel round the world to support their sons at every Test they play.

Within the Springbok set-up itself, women are scarce. There were only three in the 47-strong World Cup contingent: AnneLee, physiotherapist Rene Naylor and massage therapist Daliah Hurwitz. What's it like, I ask. Much like it is for any woman operating in a man's world, she replies. 'You have to work that bit extra – I've worked hard for fourteen years to get where I am. You have to be tough and you have to stand up to different people; you don't want to mess that up by being silly; my professional integrity is important to me and I'm not going to mess that up for anything.'

You have to maintain strict boundaries. In other words, no office romances. 'I'm very fond of the players, but they are not my friends. I go to their weddings and there will always be some players I will keep in touch with, but as professional associates.'

Like Rene Naylor, many younger women would happily

trade places with her. 'You can see why they would want my job.' What they don't see is the many stressful aspects of it. 'You work with men and you travel a lot with them and that can be very intimidating for your partner. So I keep my private life separate.'

AnneLee's job is multifaceted. As with any management member, she has to play a parental role. 'If, say, we are in Dunedin and we lose, we can't sulk. We have to deal with the hotel accounts, pack, make sure the visas are in order. The players feed a lot off you, so you have to say: "Guys, the sun will shine again tomorrow. We are a professional team. We look good and we hold our heads up high."'

* * *

On 29 September 2011, I catch the 7.50 plane from Taupo to Auckland. I'll be there for two nights for the Samoa game. Kelly Fourie and Janine Habana are on the same flight. Their respective husbands, Jaque and Bryan, are up early with them, taking them into the hotel restaurant for breakfast and then coming out to the airport shuttle to say goodbye. They and the rest of the Boks will take a chartered flight later in the morning. While we wait for the plane to arrive at the tiny Taupo airport, I chat to Kelly and Janine. Both are dainty, pretty women and sexily dressed. Janine wears boots and a miniskirt that shows off a perfectly toned figure. Twenty-four-year-old Kelly has deep blue-eyes and long black hair, capped with a jaunty brown beret. She and Jaque met through a mutual friend, she says, and were married on 30 May 2009. They struggled to find a date that fitted in with

125

Jaque's rugby commitments and ended up marrying on the same day as the Super 14 final won by the Bulls. The Lions, for whom Jaque was then playing, had fortunately already been knocked out.

After they married, she and Jaque moved to Cape Town and he joined Western Province. They have kept their properties in Johannesburg and are renting in Baronetcy estate in Plattekloof. The Habanas are neighbours.

'It's nice having the other wives here, because we do things together when the boys are training. They have the same routine as they do at home. They come home at 5 or 6pm. They have their own dinner at 7pm and have team dinner out on Tuesday or Wednesday. The only difference is that we are staying in a hotel and not at home.'

She and Jaque own 50% of a business, making diamond wedding bands. Their partners are in Johannesburg. The company is called Nightfall Diamonds. She works from home. The may own it jointly but, of course, she runs it. 'He's mostly away, and I have to work with the clients,' she says matter-of-factly. 'We have a catalogue and it's mostly word of mouth.'

I ask her how she copes with her husband's long absences. 'We have to deal with it but it's not fun. It's difficult to start a family and have a normal life. That has to be put on hold. But we make it work. We are so used to being on our own – it comes naturally. People say it's nice to have a break, but six weeks is too long. You get used to being on your own and then your husband comes back and you have to get into a routine together and then he's off again. And six weeks is a long time. I don't think people realise.'

Both she and Jaque would like children, but 'it wouldn't work until his travel slows down. We might be married but we are single mothers at the end of the day – because they aren't there.'

There is a wistfulness to Kelly Fourie. I wonder if she realised, when she married her prince – surely considered to be a hot catch – that she would end up spending most of her time alone and waiting, at the tender age of twenty-four.

Janine Habana is five years older and comes across as much more confident and in control. I tell her that I saw her and Bryan's splendid new Plattekloof home on *Top Billing* and she looks slightly embarrassed. 'We had wanted to start off smaller,' she says. It is their first marital home. 'When Bryan heard he was coming here, we flew to Cape Town to look for houses. We literally got married and moved, so it was a fresh start for us.'

Janine has a Sports Science honours degree from the University of Johannesburg. Her interest is in human movement, she says. 'We've known each other since 2001 – our second year at university – I remember him saying one day, when he's old, he will retire. I asked him what old was and he said: when he's twenty-eight!' She's amused by this. He's twenty-eight now.

'When we were in our fourth year, he got chosen for the Springboks, so made a choice to follow his dreams. I think he made the right choice.'

She, however, was equally determined. 'It was important to me to keep my own life going. It was not easy for me but I held onto it to chase my dream. And he always supported me. I always told Bryan that I had a plan. We just had to merge our plans. We support each other.' Remembering Bryan fetching his wife's laundry the night before, this made sense. This is a modern, egalitarian couple.

Her own professional life is flourishing. In Johannesburg, she has her own fitness training business. 'When I went to Cape Town, I suggested to the Institute of Fitness Professionals that I open a branch there. Now I head up the branch.

'Virgin Active is a big client, so we use their facilities. We teach you how to be a fitness trainer.'

For solace during Bryan's absences, she looks to their religious community: the Joshua Generation in Table View. 'That's like a family – and they support me a lot when Bryan is away.'

Later, I look up the Joshua Generation website. It says of itself:

> Joshua Generation Church ('Joshgen') in South Africa, is a vibrant and diverse family of God-honouring, outward-focused believers who are passionately committed to loving and serving our King and one another, and to reaching out to others by living out authentic Acts 2:42 Christianity.

I remark to Janine, after watching Bryan over this last month, that he gives an impression of centredness. Before she arrived, he pottered about the hotel, mostly on his own, looking utterly content. 'He has an inner peace,' she agrees eagerly. She has a similar air.

It impresses me how clear she is about her life, knowing

how to make the best of what she has and to get what she needs. Kids, for instance.

'I've always known I wasn't going to have kids early – from thirty I will start thinking about it. Bryan would love kids now, but we're not planning to immediately. That will be the next chapter: between thirty and forty. It's important to know what you want or life is crazy.'

I've noticed with professional rugby players that they often seem to marry women a year or so older than themselves. Presumably because they want strong women who are able to keep the home fires burning while they are off doing battle. I ask her if she worries about Bryan getting injured. Not really, she says.

'They start so young that they learn early to deal with the pressures of the industry. He gets up every morning knowing he will be doing what he loves. I'm in sports science, and I know how much they can take, so I'm not too emotional about it. They train for it. They are strong. But they do get over-use injuries, so they can't go on too long. They take so many hits that they do need to retire.'

The following year, Kelly and Jaque Fourie left for Japan, where he earned R10 million a year at the Kobelco Steelers. He plays only 13 or 14 games a year, with minimal travel, and photographs show a happy, smiling Kelly, very different from the forlorn young woman I'd met in New Zealand.

In late 2013, Janine and Bryan Habana head off to France where he will play for Toulon, building up his retirement funds. He will also gain experience of playing in northern hemisphere conditions, which will stand him in good stead for a place in the 2015 Springbok World Cup squad, a place he very much wants.

9 The Black Bok

In New Zealand, I was fascinated by how the Boks paired up in their downtime. Jaque Fourie and Francois Hougaard seemed inseparable. Jean de Villiers and Schalk Burger hung out with Butch James and Francois Louw. The white Bulls boys kept to themselves. And the black players formed a different group altogether. I thought about this one day at the InterContinental in Wellington, watching Juan de Jongh, Chiliboy Ralepelle, JP Pietersen, Odwa Ndungane and Gio Aplon, on their day off, walk down the stairs together and head out to a waiting taxi. The only thing that unites these five is that they're not white: Juan, Gio and JP are coloured and their home language is Afrikaans. Odwa and Chiliboy are black. Odwa's first language is isiXhosa. They don't share a common union: Odwa and JP are Sharks; Juan and Gio Aplon are Stormers; Chiliboy is a Bull.

In his autobiography, Victor Matfield writes about the 2003 incident that rapidly escalated to a racism-in-the-Boks scandal. 'It became apparent that Geo Cronje and Quinton Davids would have to share, even though Rudolph [sic] knew Geo wasn't comfortable with such an arrangement.' Matfield doesn't give the reason for Geo's discomfort, but it was afterwards widely reported to be his objection to sharing a room with a coloured player. Matfield reveals that Cronje then moved in with Fourie du Preez, who was sharing with Gcobani Bobo, and the two players of colour then teamed up.

Matfield justifies the swap thus: 'There are many different cultures in South Africa, and each one tends to band together with its own kind. It wasn't unusual for the Afrikaans guys in the team to seek out one other's company, and the players of colour and the English-speaking guys did the same.'

Victor also reveals that Jake White was disturbed by what he perceived to be Bulls' clannishness. 'Jake White couldn't understand why the Bulls players often wanted to do things together, in a group, and he didn't like it. We ate lunch together, we went out on the town together and we shared rooms together. For us, this was natural behaviour – as a team, we had a unique dynamic.'

He doesn't say so, but presumably he is talking only about white, Afrikaans-speaking Bulls.

So, nothing has changed in terms of affiliation in the intervening years. What occurs to me is this: that these guys are under intense pressure; they are away from their comfort zones and loved ones. Let them seek solidarity where they can. What's more, people are attracted to each other and become friends instinctively. It's not necessarily a conscious process. But I'm still puzzled.

After we returned from New Zealand, I asked one of the black Boks about his experience and got an unexpectedly passionate response – but only once he felt he trusted me sufficiently not to reveal his identity. I prefer not to do anonymous interviews, but I thought his reasons compelling enough to agree.

'There is so much that black players stomach inside,' he says, 'because, if you let it out in the media, you won't make the team. And, if you don't make the team, they will say: sorry, we can't renew your contract because you're not playing so why should we keep you? If you take on the administrators, you can kiss your career goodbye. Once they write you off, they write you off everywhere.'

This often has particular ramifications for black players. Apartheid robbed black families of the opportunity to accrue financial and social capital. A large majority are still barely edging out of poverty. Once one of their sons becomes professional, and has a job with a salary, he will be expected to help support the family. That means 'you are supporting your brothers and sisters through school'. So the cancelling of a contract blights not only the player's prospects but those of his family as well.

The black Bok – whom I'm going to refer to as BB – says that although the appointment of the first black Springbok coach in Peter de Villiers made little difference in terms of selection it made a big difference in other ways. 'With the Springboks, you get different cultures, different personalities. It's a very diverse group, so you've got to be able to handle that and bring out the best in all the players. Peter is good to the black players. He communicates with them. It's much easier for a black player to speak to someone who he feels he can relate to about what he is going through. In that sense, it was easier for black players to approach him, because we can see someone who has gone through many of the same difficulties we have gone through to get to the highest level.

'For black players, it's been tough over the years because it's a white-dominated sport. We don't have a lot of black coaches, and, you know, often your coach is a kind of mentor. Someone you can lean on, tell him when you are stressed, or whatever. It's much easier to confide in a black coach than it is to confide in a white coach, because you feel the guy can relate to what you are saying.

'Some white coaches are good in that they give you the freedom to share what you are feeling, but you don't feel comfortable to share the deep stuff. Because we all struggle to break through to senior levels – both the coach and the players – we are all going through the same thing. We hope things will change over time. It's been a bit slower than we hoped, but maybe, one day, our kids will benefit!'

He laughs at this. The hopelessness of it. He is only in his late twenties himself.

I ask him about the social segregation I see. And, at this, he becomes slightly defensive. It's clearly been raised in the team before.

'In most teams I've been involved in, it's like that,' he says. 'It's nothing against the spirit of the team. The spirit is pretty good between blacks, Afrikaans, English, coloureds, but at leisure time, when we go for coffee, the people we go for coffee with ...' He breaks off, hesitates a minute and then carries on: 'It's nothing against the Afrikaners, but what Afrikaans guys talk about might be different from what we talk about. Because most of them come from farms, and they talk about farming. Whereas we enjoy talking about soccer, or cars, or whatnot. So it's nothing to do with colour; it's more about what people associate with. So when we go out, we do share tables and have coffee with the white guys, but most of the time you just chill with those you are comfortable with. It's not race, it's just that we talk about different stuff. It's not language: everyone talks English comfortably. It's more what we talk about.'

I'm not convinced. Juan de Jongh, for instance, is not a big soccer fan. I know because I asked him. Nor is Jean de Villiers the farming type. His future is in business. I know BB was just throwing out examples, but not being white seems to me the primary attraction between these guys from very different cultures and different unions.

BB stresses that he is one of the lucky ones – he broke through the glass ceiling. But he has watched and played with many black players at provincial level who have not made it. 'I know I'm pretty blessed in relation to some other guys. I've seen guys whose contracts have not been renewed, who have been overlooked for selection. That is very frustrating for a player: when you know there is no way another guy is better than you but he gets picked ahead of you. I've had hardship too, but it's never been as bad as other people have experienced.

'People say contracts are not renewed because they don't fit into our style of play or whatever. Sometimes we have to take what they tell us, but I honestly believe there have been a few who have been overlooked because of their colour.'

It's the same in the corporate world, he says. And in other white-dominated sports, such as cricket. 'Black people are overlooked for promotion. We know we have to work twice as hard to get a look in. White coaches trust their own kind,' he says. Peter might be black, but the other five coaches – Gary Gold, Dick Muir, Rassie Erasmus, Jacques Nienaber and Percy Montgomery – are all white. 'So it's one against five. If you're outnumbered like that, there is not much you can do. So it was tough for Peter. He probably tried to push to give more black people more opportunities. So four or six of the senior players, plus some of the coaches, pick the team. They are friends. They have braais at each other's houses. So, if you are Peter, you are all on your own.

'They trust their own kind. If someone of colour comes, you have to work three times as hard as the white person for them to trust you. If you are a similar race, they will trust you. But for someone of colour, even though your record can speak for itself, every day you have to prove yourself again and again. The media plays a big part. The media can sway the public against someone big time. And, although Peter was undermined from the start [by Oregan Hoskins's comment], they are the ones who drive the public against him most of the time.

'Peter doesn't know what he's doing': this is what I keep reading! In the streets people keep asking me if Peter is doing the coaching. No one ever asked me that about Jake White! When we do the video or meet outside, the assistant coaches take over. Peter just watches. Peter does his coaching indoors. People have no idea what's going on. They just see this on TV and what they read, and they believe the worst.

'This frustrated him; he could see people were trying to bring him down and so he became defensive. He was an emotional person.'

BB believes De Villiers was better for black players than Jake White because the latter was 'obsessed with size and the look of the player rather than what the player can do. Jake overlooked a lot of good players, because if you are not a certain size, were not benching a certain weight, he would not consider you.

'Peter also had a very good rugby brain and he was very

good at analysing players and coming up with solutions. And what I liked about Peter was that he gave the team leadership more freedom, because on the field the coach is not there, you need the leaders on the field to coach and guide the team. I liked that he gave the players the freedom to run the team on the field. But, if you do that, people can undermine you, so it can come back to bite you. It is not good when the team is not supportive. You can't abuse that.'

At Bok level, there is only 10% representation of black players. 'In 2011, it shouldn't be like that. There are so many black players out there. When politicians go to the Springboks and say "Where are the black players?" they are going to the wrong place. They should go to the Cheetahs, the Sharks, the Bulls, Western Province. That is where the Springboks come from. A Springbok coach can't pick players unless they are playing for their province. You can't tell me after so many years that the provinces can only find three black players.' At the Bulls, for instance, they recruit a lot of black players in the junior levels. 'And then they frustrate them!' Because so few go on to be contracted into the senior ranks, the springboard for elevation to the national team.

Generally, he alleges, white players earn more than white players, 'right from the initial recruitment, straight from school.'

'At Springbok level, you are paid according to your number of caps. And who has more caps? The white players! Because they get more opportunity. The seniority of the players is what counts. Of course, negotiations are behind closed doors but players talk. So you know.'

BB said that, at one point in his career, he had a Kiwi coach who didn't see colour. His face lights up when he talks about this man, as if remembering a halcyon era of ease and innocence. 'It's so nice when you have a guy who backs you completely, who doesn't have hidden agendas. But, even with a foreign coach, you still have the same administrators in power.'

For John Smit, BB has nothing but praise. 'John is one of best leaders I've ever come across. The media love him today and hate him tomorrow. That made him strong. The difference between John and Peter was he did not become emotional, and then you say things you regret. John is a natural-born leader. He is fair to everyone. He treats everyone the same – whether he's a new player in the team or a senior. Whether he's black, coloured or white. John was one of the best guys I've ever played under.'

* * *

In its constitution, SARU states that its 'main object is the promotion, development and support of all levels of rugby in the Republic. SARU's ancillary objects include, but are not limited to':

5.1 applying its income, directly and indirectly, for the promotion, development, support, upliftment, administration and playing of rugby in South Africa;
5.2 pursuing policies and programmes, at national and all other levels, aimed at redressing imbalances of the past and creating a genuinely non-racial, non-political and democratic dispensation for rugby in South Africa.

Black and white rugby unions merged in 1992. So we are into our third decade of theoretically non-racial rugby. But SARU's own statistics on the progress they have made are damning. In 2012, there were six blacks, eight coloured and 14 white Springboks in the squad. But even that paltry number of blacks scarcely made an impression on the field. Chiliboy Ralepelle, for example, has now slipped back to third-choice Springbok hooker, after Bismarck du Plessis and Adriaan Strauss, and was brought on for a few minutes in the odd game and barely given a chance to show what he was worth.

But, as BB points out, judging the levels of racial progress in rugby by the colour of the national team is superficial and counterproductive. It puts unfair pressure on the national coach and the players themselves, particularly the few black players who make it through. It saps emotional energy from a team because they are forced to think of themselves in racial terms, and to compete with each other on the basis of race, when everything in the dynamics of a successful team works in the opposite direction – of seamless brotherhood, regardless of superficial differences. It seems to me quite clear now that this voluntary segregation by players of colour is all to do with this. What bonds these men is the common experience of being judged by their skin colour. No matter how hard they try, they are never certain whether they will be accepted simply as the best player or whether they will have to bear the humiliating tag of 'quota player'.

Roux's term as CEO has seen some welcome innovations: the creation of three rugby academies in Boland, East London and Port Elizabeth, paid for by a R30-million Lotto grant.

The new SARU director of rugby, Rassie Erasmus, oversees a travelling high-performance skills unit that offers crash courses to communities and schools.

But the most significant development has been the first-ever audit by SARU of exactly where rugby is played in South Africa. The figures show how many rugby clubs and rugby-playing schools there are in each so-called geo-political province, and which SARU unions fall into that province. The statistics show that 60% of all rugby-playing high schools are in the Western Cape and Eastern Cape, the provinces where black and coloured people historically favour rugby above soccer. In other words, SARU, over the two decades since the democratisation of rugby, has done nothing to extend the areas where rugby is played. And, instead of ploughing its considerable resources into these potential rugby goldmines, it is spending millions each year on propping up unions where rugby is hardly played – for example, in Mpumalanga and North West. One of the arguments that supported the existence of the small unions was that they developed rugby in the platteland, which in turn produced future Springboks. But this is no longer the case. It is individual schools that attract and nurture schoolboy talent. And, as the 2011 national census shows, urbanisation is a tremendous force in contemporary South Africa.

The last major shake-up of rugby happened in 1996, with the advent of the professional era, when Louis Luyt negotiated a historic US$555-million broadcast deal with Rupert Murdoch's News Corporation. In his 2004 autobiography, *Walking Proud*, Luyt describes the process: 'To facilitate South African rugby's bold entry into the brave new world of professionalism, we needed to drastically reduce the number of SARFU member unions from its all-time high of 23. While quite substantial, the income from News Corporation was hardly sufficient to support so many provincial unions. After tough and, at times, trying talks we ended up with 14 unions.

'The four major provinces – Transvaal, Natal, Northern Transvaal and Western Province – were each allocated R4.14 million to pay their players, while Eastern Province and Free State received R3 million each from SARFU. Griqualand West, Border and Western Transvaal were paid almost R2.5 million each and the other provincial teams – Boland, South Western Districts, Eastern Transvaal, South Eastern Transvaal and Northern Free State – each R2.24 million.'

Nothing has changed since the Luyt era. All the power in South African rugby still resides in those 14 putative strongholds, regardless of the fact that at least six of them preside over geographical areas where less and less rugby is played. What apparently influenced Luyt in his distribution of largesse was the extent to which he could count on the loyalty of the clique of men who ran each of these unions when it came to his own battles to stay in power.

It is no coincidence that several of them are clustered around Johannesburg, his seat of power: Springs, Potchefstroom, Pretoria, Kimberley, Witbank. Yet, these are not the areas where the most rugby is played. Nor have most of these unions succeeded in spreading the game in their areas in the intervening decades.

SARU mostly delegates development to its constituent unions. But the smaller unions use the millions allocated to them each year to buy in Vodacom and Currie Cup teams. The Vodacom Cup, in particular, is supposed to promote development, but most teams fielded are predominantly white.

Another major problem is that, even in some of the provinces richly endowed with rugby talent, the unions are very badly run. An example is the Border Union in East London, which has for years been a disaster zone. How can the body running South African rugby allow this to happen in such an important province for rugby? It's down to the ownership structure: no matter how useless, Border, like every other of the 14 unions that make up SARU, gets two votes, weighted equally with the giants like Western Province, the Sharks and the Bulls.

One of the best performing schools in the area controlled by the Border Union is Dale College in King William's Town. I went to Dale in August 2010 for the annual derby between Dale and its main rival, Queen's College, another top Eastern Cape school. Dale left a deep impression on me. An all-boys' school, and over 90% black, it has a rugby culture similar to that of Grey College and Paarl Gim. At the primary school, all 400 boys play rugby at every available opportunity – at breaks, after school, on weekends. Teachers told me that, if they needed to punish a boy, all they had to do was threaten to take away his rugby for a week.

At the senior school, which has close on 600 boys, it is a similar story. The passion and the talent are there in abundance. What Dale needs to become a significant incubator of Springboks like Grey College and Paarl Gim is a similar lavishing of resources. But most of the boys come from poor, single-parent families. Their diet consists of bread or pap (porridge) three times a day. There is very little of the protein crucial to the building of muscle, particularly in the adolescent years. Poverty deprives these boys of a shot at the big time simply because they don't get enough to eat. And the South African game favours big, strong players.

Grey College and Paarl Gim each have a dedicated rugby staff: a director of rugby, conditioning coaches, biokineticists, physiotherapists and state-of-the-art equipment. Dale's rugby coaches double as teachers and as surrogate fathers. There is a small, basic gym. And that's it. Grant Griffiths, first-team coach in 2010, drove boys to and from their homes for practice and games because they couldn't afford taxis. He'd buy them rugby boots and feed them out of his own somewhat meagre salary. I wrote about this in my last book, *Touch, Pause, Engage!*, naively assuming it would spark outrage and shame SARU into doing something.

In 2013, I phoned Mike Eddy, principal of Dale College, expecting to find an improvement. No, he said, all that had changed was that Grant Griffiths had been poached by Cape Town's Hamiltons rugby club. And one of their former pupils has been signed by the Southern Kings, which is a step forward, because at least he doesn't have to leave the Eastern Cape. Otherwise, the struggle continues. Their best players are still being lured away by richer unions in other provinces and they still struggle to find the cash to pay coaches.

The only connection they have with Border Union is that one of their coaches comes up to Dale to help out in his free time – but he does it as a personal favour and Dale has to pay him out of school funds.

The only sponsorship they get is R40 000 from FNB every

Tendai (Beast) Mtawarira, SARU PR and Admin Manager AnneLee Murray and Morné Steyn.

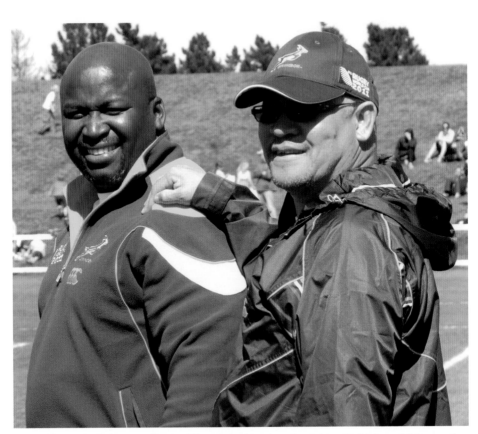

Also at Taupo, logistics guru Charles Wessels is shown on the right, with Malome Maimane, the Springbok technical analyst, who has since tragically died.

Massage therapist Daliah Hurwitz (left) and physiotherapist Rene Naylor (right) watch training at Taupo.

Physiotherapist Vivian Verwant works on Danie Rossouw during a Taupo training session.

Janine Habana (left) and Kelly Fourie (right) about to board an Air New Zealand flight from Taupo to Auckland to watch their husbands play Samoa (29 September 2011).

During the 2011 Rugby World Cup, ardent fans Andre Fortman (from PE) and Francois van Zyl (from Robertson) trailed the Boks round New Zealand in a freezing camper van. Here, in Taupo, they had just got lucky. An Afrikaans family had invited them home for a hot shower and a meal.

At Ekhaya, the hospitality centre set up by the South African government in the Amora Hotel in Wellington, Bryan Habana and Peter de Villiers have just handed over a Springbok jersey, signed by all the players, to be auctioned off to raise funds for victims of the February 2011 Christchurch earthquake.

On 7 October 2011, at the Amora Hotel: Jean de Villiers, backs coach Dick Muir and Victor Matfield at the last press conference before the fateful game against the Australians.

The last photograph of Peter de Villiers's 2011 Rugby World Cup team, taken at the Amora Hotel in Wellington (8 October 2011).

A devastated John Smit and Peter de Villiers at the media conference at the Wellington Stadium after the Springboks' ejection from the 2011 Rugby World Cup.

Jean de Villiers and Siya Kolisi lift the 2012 Currie Cup. Injury kept them out of the final, but both contributed hugely to the team's success throughout the year.

Charles Wessels choreographs the team photo of Heyneke Meyer's 2012 Bok squad, in the gardens of the Montecasino Hotel in Johannesburg, before the game against the All Blacks at the FNB Stadium on 5 October. The All Blacks won the game 16–32.

The long and the short of it: Peter de Villiers consoles John Smit, that morning castigated in the New Zealand media for pinching a silver fern from a pub garden during a road trip with several Boks from Auckland back to Taupo after the pool game against Namibia during the 2011 Rugby World Cup (24 September 2011).

other year when they host a Classic Clash with their arch-rival, Queen's College, another Eastern Cape school that produces large numbers of black rugby players without any help from SARU.

Dale cannot afford to employ a full-time rugby coach. They had to construct a package in order to provide employment for Luke Smith, their current coach. This includes the job of buildings administrator.

But, as Eddy points out, that is only part of it. In 2010, Dale had a matric pass rate of 98%, which makes it highly sought after in a dysfunctional province with an average pass rate of 58%. To get their sons in, many parents give local addresses. Only once school starts does it become obvious that they actually live much further away, many in Mdantsane, outside East London, which entails a 50km journey each way by taxi. More often than not, they arrive late. After-school activities become problematic. The entire ecosystem in which Dale operates makes schooling a challenge.

With minimal resources, Dale not only keeps its own teams going, but it also provides a development programme for four surrounding poorer schools.

Eddy lists the problems in a matter-of-fact way, not complaining, but expressing gratitude for the bits of help the school does get.

Nevertheless, it is an indictment of SARU.

It is clear from SARU's own research that Western and Eastern Cape schools are the richest source of black players. Dale is extremely well run. It has the facilities, the talent and the passion. Why doesn't SARU invest some of its budget here? Provide top coaches, a proper gym and a budget for touring? Both Dale junior and senior schools have very good hostels, where boys get three balanced meals a day. It costs R38 000 a year for board and tuition for each boy. Why not sponsor a generous number of them so that the crucial problem of poor nutrition is sorted, as is the issue of transport to training and games?

The failure to fund this kind of development and the focus instead on racial inequity at higher levels leads to other distortions. What happens now is that richer unions poach promising black players from poor Eastern Cape schools and put them into the schools that offer the kind of facilities that Dale cannot. So a boy from King William's Town is plucked from his family and sent to Pretoria Boys High or Glenwood or Michaelhouse. Their parents, faced with offers of full bursaries at these very good schools, capitulate. But frequently the boys struggle.

Stormers hooker Siyabonga Ntubeni studied at Dale until Grade 9, when he moved to King Edward VII High School in Johannesburg, because, as he rightly calculated, KES offered him a better springboard to get into professional rugby.

Ntubeni grew up in King William's Town and has played rugby all his life: 'As little kids, we would fill a plastic bottle with sand and pretend it was a rugby ball and play in the streets till the street lights went on. That was the signal to drop the ball and run home because otherwise we would be in trouble.' In the hostel at Dale, they played rugby at break time, after school and before bedtime.

The move to KES was difficult. 'I went from small town to big city and totally different demographics: from predominantly black to predominantly white; from not-so-stable families to wealthy families. But I adapt quickly. There were very good people at KES and I had a lot of support.' The husband of one of his teachers mentored him then and still does.

But he watched as other kids from the Eastern Cape struggled to adapt, many of them giving up and returning home after only a few months. What sets Ntubeni apart and, presumably, gives him added emotional resilience is that he grew up in a strong, cohesive family with two employed and engaged parents.

Talking to him, I get a different impression from that of BB. Perhaps it is the fact that Ntubeni is almost a decade younger and race relations have improved so rapidly in the past ten years, with new cohorts of kids emerging from mixed schools with no direct experience of apartheid's racial hierarchies and divisions. Or is it the fact that he plays his rugby at Western Province, under a black coach? Ntubeni hates any reference to race. For him, the most hurtful slur possible is to label him a quota player. He just wants to be seen as a player.

In 2012, Ntubeni shared a house with Siyamthanda Kolisi across the road from Newlands stadium. The house is owned by Western Province Rugby Union, and they lived under the watchful eye of their agent, Paul van der Berg.

Close though the two are, Kolisi strikes me as having been the more vulnerable boy. He did not have the advantage of secure parenting, having been born to teenage parents in Port Elizabeth's Zwide township, and was brought up in poverty by his grandmother. While he was still at primary school, a local coach recognised his talent, and, on this basis, he won a bursary to Grey High School in Port Elizabeth.

I interviewed him the day after Western Province won the 2012 Currie Cup – for the first time in over a decade. The arrangement was that I would pick him at the Newlands house. To my surprise, Paul also got into the car. He was going to sit in on the interview. This was the first time I had ever had to conduct an interview in the presence of an agent. At the Slug & Lettuce pub in Main Road, Kolisi asked for a blanket to wrap around him because, even though it was late spring, he was cold. Although injury had prevented Kolisi from taking part in the final, he had contributed significantly to the team's success all year and had celebrated with them into the early hours of that morning. He was still suffering from the after-effects.

My plan had been to track Kolisi's roots back to Zwide, to do a case study similar to what I had done with the Du Plessis brothers and Jean de Villiers, because the conditions in which this particular Springbok had been reared were so very different from – and so much harder than – theirs. But I had reckoned without the ubiquitous agent. I needed permission from the head office, he said. This was strange, I pointed out. I had never had to go through an agent to interview any other player. Agents take a cut of players' earnings and answer to them, not the other way round.

Kolisi, sitting there shivering in his blanket, was drinking glass after glass of water in an attempt to rehydrate. He hated going back to the township, he said, because, once he was there, everyone wanted a piece of him. It was what drove him repeatedly to put his body on the line. 'I don't care what happens to me,' he said. 'Because, if I don't play, people in the township don't eat.'

Jacques Nienaber had said to me that the only other player he had seen with the same hunger as the Du Plessis brothers was Siya Kolisi. All three were driven by need. It seemed a dreadful burden for someone so young, and it bore out what BB had told me about black players. I was more than ever determined to explore his origins. What had this boy had to overcome to get to where he was? And what demons would he need to battle to make it to the highest level?

The very next day, I arrived at the agent's office and was given the brushoff. No, it was not allowed.

The most effective – and dispassionate – mentoring Siya Kolisi gets is from Jean de Villiers. In the week leading up to Kolisi's Springbok debut in the 2013 Rugby Championship game against Scotland in Mbombela (Nelspruit), De Villiers shared a room with Kolisi. Any Bok with more than 50 caps is entitled to his own room, a cherished privilege which De Villiers voluntarily gave up in order to give Kolisi as much support as possible in the fraught build-up to the biggest game of his life. It paid off: Kolisi played brilliantly and was named man of the match. This not only demonstrates the mettle of the Bok captain but also how far the team has come in the decade since the room-sharing scandal of 2003.

Keith Richardson is the veteran headmaster of Wynberg Boys' High School in Cape Town, another excellent state school and one that 'churns out black boys'. He says all his experience points to the crucial role of parents – and particularly fathers – in the successful nurturing of boys.

This puts most black boys at a disadvantage. 'Eighty per cent of them either have absentee fathers or no fathers in their lives at all. They are brought up by their mothers or grandmothers.'

But a father, he says, 'is everything'. Boys unconsciously mimic their fathers' behaviour. 'If you have a father who is racist or abusive, say, to beggars at street lights, the sons will do the same. A father who is abusive at the edge of the field and rants at the coach or ref during a game sets that example to his son. A father needs to have a balanced approach. He needs to be at a boy's side when he is winning and when he is losing.' I thought, as he was speaking, of Francois du Plessis and Andre de Villiers. These are the kinds of father a boy needs.

The residual effects of apartheid also make things harder for black boys. Their parents themselves are frequently uneducated, and few are middle class, with the confidence and social capital that brings. 'The next generation will be different,' he says. The boys brought into the system now will be able to pass what they have received onto their children. Every boy who enrols at Wynberg is allocated a mentor. Most are boarders: 'It takes a special kind of boy to go back to the township in his school shorts and come here to school every day.'

To a much lesser extent, Richardson faces the same problem as Mike Eddy at Dale College. Richer, private schools try to buy their promising black rugby players. It's a pernicious system, because frequently this happens in Grade 11. Schools don't want to be saddled with a boy who doesn't perform, so they recruit him to provide the X-factor to their first teams in the last two years of school. A boy in this position frequently faces hostility from existing pupils, because he is given the place in the team the incumbent has worked for throughout his school career.

For the black boy, being catapulted into a new school, particularly a much richer school, for the last two years of his school career is also bound to affect his academic achievements. And, because he has been admitted to the elite institution purely to boost their rugby team, if he doesn't perform he is made to feel a failure.

This cynical use of young boys speaks to the power of rugby. A school whose first team performs well at rugby is considered a good school, no matter what its other weaknesses. Parents with resources flock to such schools. Old boys open their wallets more eagerly. Greater resources mean schools can employ more teachers than the government will pay for, which means smaller classes and more individual attention. They can afford playing fields, libraries, computer labs, swimming pools – and directors of rugby.

The ideal solution to this, of course, lies in strengthening schools in traditionally black areas so that kids are not wrenched away from home, but can get the best teachers and coaches at a local school. My mind keeps going back to Dale College. All they need is a bit of help.

10 The Banker

I first heard of Louis von Zeuner in September 2010 when news broke of an SMS he had sent to Oregan Hoskins, president of SARU. The SMS – or the part of the SMS that made the media – reads: 'Regan, I think you should write to the major unions on black players – judging from today's games Lions 2, Bulls 1, Cheetahs 2 – they are not respecting the spirit and goals of transformation – Louis.'

Von Zeuner was deputy CEO of ABSA, which sponsors the Currie Cup, as well as the Springboks and the Sevens team. The SMS came shortly after the Currie Cup final on 11 September 2010.

Oregan Hoskins duly wrote to the unions – representing it as a sponsor requirement, rather than a SARU one – and the exchange was leaked. AfriForum went ballistic, launching a campaign called 'Stop ABSA Quotas' and threatening a mass boycott of the bank, which it accused of political interference in sport.

Solidarity chief executive Flip Buys wrote an open letter to Maria Ramos, CEO of ABSA, which included the statement that Solidarity 'are perturbed about the manner in which ABSA is neglecting its traditional support base and Afrikaans speakers in particular'.

Two things are interesting here. Firstly, nowhere in his SMS did Louis mention quotas. Secondly, Buys responded to ABSA's call for more representivity with his own call for more attention to be paid to Afrikaans-speakers. In other words, he played up race and harked back to a time when Afrikaners were privileged. Special pleading, therefore, for a specific racial grouping – exactly what they were attacking ABSA for.

The reactionary nature of this intervention was reflected in the racist drivel that dominated the comments following online media reports. It's always been a revelation to me – and a relief – to see how much more enlightened and progressive most professional rugby players are by comparison with some of their fans.

Such was the personal vitriol directed at Louis von Zeuner that he had to get protection for his family. But he never for a second backed down.

Recalling the furore for me, he says AfriForum's accusation that he called for quotas doesn't make sense. 'It's crazy to think that any sponsor would support a structure whereby people or players aren't selected on merit, and that at the end of the day you can have players in a team that are just not up to it. I also understand that, if all else fails, you can be forced to do that and that was my concern at that time. The example that I used with Regan Hoskins was, if a union like the Bulls, on a particular Saturday only has the ability to put one player of colour into their most senior team, then somewhere there's a problem. There's a problem either in your transformation programme or the structures that you have in place to bring people through.

'The point I made was that, if you look at some of these school tournaments, there is no shortage of talent. I used the *Beeld* Trophy as an example, where it was a school in Tzaneen that won it and the bulk of the team was of colour. In some of the central regions, again, if you look at the composition of these school teams, there's an abundance of talent. So our structures from school on need to be of the nature that we can push through talent. If the make-up of the most senior team shows that you can't have that, then there's something wrong and we need to address that.

'We have never been prescriptive on anything! But what I did say to SA Rugby was that, in their constitution, they refer to their support of transformation and everything that comes with it, and I said, in the spirit of good governance, in the spirit of the service level agreement we have with you – based on your constitution, not on anything that we've prescribed – we need to do this. The only thing that we, as a sponsor, want at the end of the day is a full house.

'The example I used was that you were able to draw 94 000 people to Soccer City for a Test, and just the weekend thereafter the Boks played at Loftus and we couldn't fill the stadium. And, and my issue is, what will fill a stadium is interest in the game, people who want to see their heroes, their role models or people who want to see family or friends on the pitch. You need to take a step back, evaluate all of that. Where are we coming short, where is something not working? And what should we do?'

'That is my fight with my Afrikaans friends. [I say] "I'm no less Afrikaans than you, I'm no less Christian than you, but it is more important to me that my children operate in a normal society than it is [to give in to] your onslaught against me." There must be equal opportunity for everyone who wants to get involved in the game – fairness to everyone, regardless of race. If I can't say that, then I must step away because I'm not living my value system.'

Sitting opposite Von Zeuner on the eighth floor of ABSA Towers in downtown Johannesburg, I think: so this is where the grown-ups in national rugby are! The guys who pay the bills. Who are rooted in reality yet have a clear vision of where things should be heading. And he runs a multibillion-rand business on the side.

I have banked with ABSA for the past ten years, but grudgingly, mainly because I think they fleece me with incomprehensible bank charges. But, listening to Louis, I begin to think it is, after all, money well spent. ABSA is the Springboks' main sponsor. Over a five-year period, they will pump hundreds of millions of rands into the Boks.

ABSA itself has undergone cataclysmic changes in culture and vision in order to survive and grow. One of its founding institutions was Volkskas, a bank formed by the Broederbond in 1934 and whose first chairman was also chair of the secretive Afrikaner supremacist organisation. ABSA was formed in the 1990s as an amalgamation of the Volkskas and Allied banks and UBS. Today, two thirds of ABSA's customers are not white. As I listen to Louis von Zeuner describe the way ABSA has evolved in order to keep up with changing times and to meet changing demands, it strikes me that business at its best is a progressive force. And rugby is being dragged along in its wake because it has to reflect the changing face of its paymaster. And a very good thing that is, too, because, I suspect, if left to its own devices, rugby would eventually dwindle into a theme park for those who yearn for a lost era.

I'm sure one can't boil these things down to an individual,

but it does seem to me that Louis von Zeuner has personally had a lot of influence. A former player, he combines a passion for rugby with a first-class banker's brain. A heavy-set man, he appears as Afrikaans as they come. His English is good but not perfect, his manner is considered and deliberate. His driver conveys him to and from Pretoria, where he lives. He was late for our meeting: the traffic was particularly bad, he explains. Waiting for him to arrive, I had told his PA that I had a meeting scheduled immediately afterwards with Imtiaz Patel, head of MultiChoice, at his office in Randburg. I didn't want to cut short my hour with Louis, but I also didn't want to be late for Imtiaz. She has evidently conveyed this to Louis because, shortly after I sit down with him, he offers to sort things out with Imtiaz for me. He taps out an SMS and reads it to me: 'I have taken up too much of Liz's time. Blame the whites!' And sends it with a grin. They have an ongoing banter about the race thing, he says.

One of Von Zeuner's early postings was at Stellenbosch, a rugby heartland. He developed a relationship with the area's rugby elite and initiated the bank's sponsorship of the first team at Paul Roos Gymnasium, the first time the school had allied itself with a commercial enterprise.

'After that, I really travelled the country. I was transferred to almost every large city in the country and the network of customers just grew and, with that an engagement with sport at all different levels.' He was offered a seat on the board of SARU, 'but we thought that was treading a fine line of getting too close, but in the process what was then established was an advisory group to SARU, myself and Trevor Munday. So, that is fifteen years of a very close relationship with the administration, with the players and with the game at large.'

In other words, he has a deep and intimate understanding of the power relations within South African rugby, so he is a man worth listening to.

The excuse that there is no black talent available doesn't wash with him. He's been there and knows that is not the problem. 'There are heavily specialised positions within a bank – such as the treasury or risk management – and every now and again we also get confronted by people that say: the talent is just not available. Well, surprise, surprise, the talent is available! What you need to do is to work harder to identify the talent; you need to make sure that your organisation attracts talent and invests in their development. You must create opportunity!

'In a large organisation, your power lies in your diversity, and what we try and drive home all the time is, whether it's business or sport, the fundamentals, the principles are exactly the same.'

Von Zeuner says he is close to the Bok team and he spoke to them just before they left for the World Cup. He used the fact that some of the senior players were retiring from rugby and going into business. 'I said: in a business you've got shareholders and they're extremely demanding. Your shareholder in sport is the public out there who buys the ticket to come and see you. My shareholder wants a monetary dividend. Yours wants a dividend that equals hope: if the Boks win on a Saturday everyone is excited and in a good mood. When you lose, you're useless; you should have been gone; you're not relevant any more. And it is exactly the same with us and that's the message that we try to drive in our engagement with SARU, with the unions, with the players. Guys, these are the fundamentals of the game today, whether your game is sport or whether your game is business. Whether I work with 40 000 employees in ABSA or you as a rugby union work with 1 000 players in your province, in your schools or whatever. It's actually no different.'

Of course, the millions ABSA hands out to South African rugby is not a charitable donation. It is a carefully calculated investment, and its efficacy as a marketing tool is constantly assessed. The bank wants to hang onto its white customers, of course, but much of the potential growth is among black people.

'In our engagement with SA Rugby, we want to make sure that the game gets presented, played and administered in a way that our customer base can associate with. We've got the largest customer base of the South African banks, and our view is that our customer base is reflective of the real South African population, from deepest rural to the most wealthy.'

Von Zeuner, like Nick Mallett, believes Test tickets are too expensive. 'I think you need to be realistic. If you are asking a ticket price of R450, that is R2 000 for a family outing for four people. It's ridiculous to think South Africans can afford that.' But radio broadcasts of games and rebroadcasts on the SABC reveal substantial interest in the game among black people, he says. Coupled with healthy sales of Bok merchandise bearing the ABSA name, this more than justifies their investment.

'We had a few cases where, at some of the stadiums, we felt that the behaviour of people wasn't always in line with making everyone feel welcome at an event, and the union took immediate steps to address that, and we welcome the fact that they did.' This would have been in 2010, around the time of his SMS to Hoskins, when the Bulls, after one too many incidents of white racists insulting black people at Loftus, took decisive action, presumably as a result of ABSA's intervention. Now, at Loftus, a sign flashes up on the big screen, giving an SMS number, which will immediately summon security if any fans become abusive.

Increasingly, says Von Zeuner, SA Rugby is taking on board this paradigm: that sport needs to follow the same principles as business. 'This has started to resonate with much of the rugby administration at a SARU level and we will check decision-making with one another.' I imagine that the checking of decision-making goes one way only, though. I can't see this international banking giant needing much advice from SARU.

This was how the controversial process of appointing Heyneke Meyer came about. Historically, the post of Springbok coach was advertised. This time, SARU kept control, drawing up a shortlist of those they considered eligible. There was much public fury about this. Von Zeuner explains the process behind it: 'I saw one of the [newspaper] headlines [claiming] that it wasn't a transparent process. Now that was a discussion that we had. If ABSA tomorrow appoints a senior executive in the group, we're not going to advertise that position. In terms of your succession planning, for business continuity, you have to know who your successors are. So, if you want to test the water and see what is out there in terms of talent, you will do it, but otherwise you won't.

'Now SARU is a business: do you tell me that you don't know who your next coach should be in terms of your strategy, where you want to get to, the game that you want to play? So you can advertise the position, but that is really just playing to the pavilion so you can say you have advertised it. You create expectations with people that you know won't be met.

'So that's a discussion we had with SARU. We said: "Guys, it doesn't work that way. At the end of the day you can tick all the boxes in a process that, possibly from a legal perspective and a technical perspective, was done phenomenally well, but if, in November of 2011, with your existing coach's contract expiring at the end of December or whenever, you don't know who the next coach should be, there isn't any strategic planning happening there."'

Von Zeuner, I have to say, is an easy man to interview. I ask a question and he instantly responds with very full, insightful answers. I feel a sense of relief here, in this unlikeliest of settings: the boardroom of that most conservative of institutions, a bank. Finally, I have the feeling that there is someone in charge: someone who has thought through all the issues in a principled, intelligent, far-sighted way. This is the first time I have felt that. And the last place I would have expected to find it.

I tell him about my conversation with BB, and how strongly he felt that black players at any level had to work twice as hard as white players to be recognised. I ask Von Zeuner what he thinks.

He takes it back to his bank experience. 'If you engage with middle management in any large corporate, they will give you exactly that feedback. In ABSA, let's take a simple example: a branch with 100 people and management of that branch being predominantly white. The teller population of that branch [would be] majority African. Where our biggest disconnect at the moment is that, at certain levels of management, decisions get made at the hand of past experience or the individual's interpretation of certain things.

'We do an employee opinion survey every second year. One of the questions we ask staff is whether they think our products are world class or the best – I can't recall the exact question. White staff will respond yes, absolutely. African staff, they say, no, they aren't. Why? White staff assess products as: Have I got access to mortgage finance, to auto finance? Have I got a cheque account and internet banking? For the African staff member, the reference is: Is cash available for somebody to take a taxi in the morning at six to get to work? And can I get access to cash if, this evening at eight o'clock on my return home, I need to quickly stop to buy this or that? Can I use the product on my mobile phone because I don't have a land line at home or, because of the digital divide, I don't have internet?'

The point of this is that if your management team represents only one segment of society – middle-aged white people, for instance – you will make decisions based on your experience, which is necessarily limited. Your organisation becomes an old boys' club – narrow, self-affirming and ultimately static and stunted. This, says Von Zeuner, applies as much to SARU as it does to a corporate.

The key, he says, is dynamism in management structures. 'In ABSA, we've really made a concerted effort to transform our executive committee. If you had looked at our executive committee in 2011, it was well diversified by race, by gender etc, but there were still blockages in our system in middle management. Because it is in middle management where you unfortunately sit with that layer of staff in the age group of forty to fifty-five and where we don't get enough young blood coming into those structures.'

That's a challenge everywhere, he says. ABSA has an out in its tie-up with banking giant Barclays. 'We are excited about the opportunity that we now have in managing Barclays on the African continent. We can now start moving talent around and possibly create space by moving people to African countries where they can further their career, but we can create an inflow of new talent into the South African business.

'So I can fully relate to what the players say to you, but I think it's the structure of society that needs to change so that those issues can be addressed.'

He says he notes how, when Heyneke Meyer and Jurie Roux are asked in the media about transformation, 'they will say, absolutely, we support transformation, and then they will say, but the best players must come through and we all agree with that'.

We're in a period of transition, he says.

'You saw how people reacted when we made our statement about transformation. SARU don't want to be exposed to that, but unfortunately those are the issues that you need to work with. What players of colour are experiencing I do think is real, but I think we should also look at where we have come from. Where are we today? Are we making progress?

And, yes, we are. Progress might be too slow but, you know, if you take Bryan Habana, Juan de Jongh, JP Pietersen, I wonder whether there's anyone in South Africa today who questions whether they are there on merit. If you look at the Springbok Sevens squad, Cecil Afrika is a hero for all South Africans. And I don't think that's where we were ten years ago.'

So, SARU appoints a black coach, a black president and vice president to show the politicians they are serious about change. 'The fact is the change happens at the middle management layer. That's where people, through a different approach, with a different engagement model, start pushing that integration.'

I know that the Boks have been through diversity workshops. The resentment from the black guys is not against their white team-mates. It is the administrators they blame. And they're right, of course.

Von Zeuner says diversity workshops have limited value. 'Man, we've exhausted that. We've had diversity workshops like it's going out of fashion, and, you know, you take people to Constitutional Hill and the Apartheid Museum, but the fact is that [black] people must get a voice.

'You know, when I look at the composition of the management team of our business bank – which is a structure that's not visible to you – they're all white. Now, if you assess ABSA [for BEE ratings], you're going to say: board transformed, exco transformed. Sixty-five per cent of my people here are of colour and race and language and whatever the case might be. But where do the decisions get made? In that management team! And that management team hasn't transformed.'

'Yesterday, I sat with the return we need to put in for a financial services charter. What do they measure us on? Top management, board, executive management. I'm going to score well on all those three structures. Does that mean that this is a transformed business? No. Because, if we talk about performance appraisals of our staff, it is that management team that determines the standards for performance. What are those standards? You need to be at work at eight o'clock in the morning. Now if I can start understanding that I am not dealing with people who necessarily have the luxury that I have to get into a car with a driver and come to work; they're dependent on a taxi. Today they strike, tomorrow the cables are stolen and the Gautrain can't work, whatever the case might be, and if this decision-making body can't understand that, at the end of the day, there are certain criteria that possibly are not relevant anymore. We are not compromising on outcome, but we can still reach this outcome with different standards.'

He reveals that he 'had a quick word with Heyneke Meyer' the other day. He should have a black player like Beast (Tendai Mtawarira) in the senior circle. 'Even if in the first six months he doesn't say a word, that's how you build capacity. Make sure your inner circle of players is representative.'

Von Zeuner had recently announced his retirement from his position as deputy CEO of ABSA. He will now serve as a non-executive director and devote time to mentoring the next generation of top bankers.

From what he tells me, this is completely his decision – nothing, as has been reported, to do with meddling by Barclays, which owns 51% of ABSA. He's acting on principle.

And, from what I've seen of him, this rings true. He's been there for thirty-two years, he says. It is time for him to move aside and let a new generation move into the seat of power. He is leading by example. SARU would do well to follow.

'I think we're heading in that direction with rugby structures, but I don't think we're there totally, and unfortunately it is back to the top. It's great to have Regan [Hoskins] in, it's great to have Mark Alexander in the structures [both are men of colour], but, if you look at the presidents of the different unions and you look at the structure where presidents can swing a vote, that shows you haven't changed, and, if you don't change that General Council and the power they have, they're going to blackball you every time.

'I mean, five unions bring in 80% of the revenue, but in decision-making the 20% of the unions can swing the vote. It's wrong.'

11 Marketing

Victor Matfield writes in his autobiography that he found media conferences stressful. 'You were only ever allowed to say what was safe. You couldn't voice your disapproval of the referee, or SARU or the International Rugby Board, because that was not in line with the "spirit of the game". You always had to be diplomatic, even when you were itching to tell the truth or voice your own opinion ...'

At the last media appearance Matfield made as Springbok captain – the final World Cup pool game, against Samoa, on 30 September 2011 – he allowed himself a bit of leeway. 'I was proud of the guys,' he said. 'They didn't give in to their shit.' It might not have been an officially sanctioned description of the opposition's behaviour, but it was an accurate one.

It was a make-or-break game for the island nation: a win would have kept them in for the quarters. A loss would send them home the following day. To add even more pressure, the game was played on the second anniversary of a tsunami that swept across Samoa and Tonga, washing away several villages and killing 189. It was a painful day for the players, and for their country, and a win might cheer people up. The Samoans were desperate to stay in the campaign, and their pent-up grief brought a wild edge to the game.

The Boks keep control in the first half. Habana scores a try in the ninth minute, converted by Morné Steyn. The Samoans are in a belligerent mood. It is clear they are targeting our ball-carriers, Schalk Burger and Heinrich Brüssow. There are several little flare-ups between Schalk and the Samoans; each time, it looks explosive, as if it could easily escalate into mass fisticuffs. But each time, he withdraws, holding up his hands, in the iconic gesture of surrender, incidentally making his innocence quite clear to the ref.

In the 25th minute, Frans Steyn belts across a penalty from an extraordinary 60m distance. Two minutes later, Morné Steyn kicks over another. By half-time, the score is 13-0.

God knows what is said in the Samoan change room at half-time, but they come back on like a team possessed, charging repeatedly at the Bok lines, barely keeping their aggression legal. Habana goes off and Hougaard comes on. I watch the discreet communication going on off-field: Charles Wessels constantly talking to the coaches on his radio, conveying information to Craig Roberts and to Percy Montgomery and Derik Coetzee, who are the official water-carriers. When they run onto the field with the water, they repeat the coach's messages to the players. In the 51st minute, George Stowers makes it across the tryline for Samoa. The score is 13-5, and it stays like that until the final whistle blows, although there is more drama in between.

Hougaard is injured and Jean de Villiers is finally on the field, the first time since he went off injured in the first game of the campaign. Paul Williams loses it and slaps Heinrich Brüssow across the face. Referee Nigel Owens gives him a red card. With 13 minutes to go, Mahonri Schwalger is denied a try through a knock-on. The crowd boos as Smit comes on in the 69th minute and Bismarck trudges off. But Smit has been on for only two minutes when Owens gives him a yellow card. For the last ten minutes, both sides play with only 14 men. Schalk is man of the match.

It wasn't a pretty game. Although we had 53% of territory, we had possession only 45% of the time. We lost three of our line-outs and had to make 152 tackles while they made only 77. But at least we now have a clear run to the knockout stage.

The Samoans have left their mark, though. Frans Steyn has sustained a campaign-ending injury to his shoulder. He will be on the next plane home. Fortunately, Jean de Villiers's rib has healed sufficiently to allow him to step seamlessly back into his old starting position.

The end of the game signals the start of the media scrum. With the other journalists, I head for a specially erected marquee beside the stadium for the post-match media conference: first with the losing captain and coach and then, after a brief interval, with the victorious captain and coach. This is followed by another media session called the 'mixed zone'. This entails forty-odd print, broadcast and digital media people from all over the world being shepherded into a wide concrete corridor, divided down the middle by waist-high railings. Selected players from both teams are then brought in and the journalists thrust tape recorders, iPhones and mics at the player they are interested in. It's a feeding frenzy, with the players corralled behind bars, safe from the barrage of journalists hungry for a usable quote.

The Boks file in one by one: Victor Matfield, Peter de Villiers, Willem Alberts, Jaque Fourie, Jean de Villiers, JP Pietersen. They have showered and changed into crisp white shirts, black pants and shoes and their Springbok blazers. Their hair has been styled – Jaque's and Jean's into spiky crests, Victor's smoothed back from his forehead into shiny black curls. They have a slightly dazed look, all the battering anger of the last 80 minutes washed and smoothed away as they rattle off an acceptable narrative. Some are more popular than others. Matfield is a star attraction, as is Jean de Villiers, who always has a large group of journalists around him because his English is good and he is articulate and witty. Shy Willem Alberts is less so. Some of the South African journalists try to keep the exchanges in Afrikaans so as to preserve a measure of exclusivity.

There is a lone Samoan: prop Census Johnston. Unlike the Boks, he looks as if he has come straight off the field. His long black hair hangs in a greasy tangle. A threadbare white towel is draped around his shoulders like an old lady's shawl. The national emotion around the anniversary of the tsunami weighed on them, he says. 'The mood of the country is dependent on how we do.' They must be feeling pretty depressed, then. This is the end of the road for the Samoans. Tomorrow they will be on the plane home.

＊ ＊ ＊

In South Africa, the public face of rugby is largely concentrated in the hands of one organisation, the media giant Naspers. Naspers owns 85% of satellite TV operator Multi-Choice, SuperSport's parent company. Naspers also owns Media24, which includes Sport24 and the most influential rugby newspapers: *Rapport, Beeld, Die Burger*. It also owns my publisher, Jonathan Ball (though no one, either at Jonathan Ball or Naspers, has ever made any attempt to influence what I write). By far the most influential of these outlets is SuperSport.

In 2011, the research company Repucom produced some interesting statistics. Outside of special occasions such as a World Cup, more than 90% of rugby games are broadcast exclusively on SuperSport, although fewer than a third of rugby fans have access to it. The long-term consequences for this are worrying, as the profile of the typical DStv consumer – at least, the one who buys the full package, the only one that includes all rugby games – represents a dwindling demographic. Fifty-one per cent of people who watch rugby on SuperSport channels are over the age of fifty; 80% of them are white; almost 70% are Afrikaans-speakers. Only a fifth of South Africans are interested in rugby, compared with soccer, which is followed by one in two South Africans.

Just under 9% of South Africans are white, so the potential for growth lies in the black market. For its own survival, rugby needs to grow markets among black communities. And growth there is potentially explosive. The most interesting recent development is the extraordinary growth in the sales of DStv's compact bouquet in the LSM 5-6 market. The compact bouquet offers only SuperSport 3 and 4, Blitz, ESPN and Tellytrack and costs R199 a month. But LSM 5 and 6 represents mostly young black people, earning around R5 000 a month, who are poised to break into the more affluent middle classes, who can afford the full package.

Viewing patterns from the World Cup appear to show that the appetite for rugby is enormous, once people get access to it. The SABC broadcast 29 games, for which they had an average audience of 1.345 million. SuperSport 1 broadcast

48 games, which were watched by a mere 242 026 on average. SuperSport 4 broadcast 26 games, with an average audience of 80 000. The final, in which South Africa didn't even feature, was viewed on SABC 2 by 73% of the combined audience average for all channels. Only 10% of viewers who had access to DStv watched the final on SABC 2.

It's possible that having a coloured man, in Peter de Villiers, as the face of South African rugby helped spread the appeal of the game among other race groups. The fact that we went into the World Cup as reigning world champions, and with the full and open support of the ANC and the government, also helped. What struck me in New Zealand was how many black South Africans had made the long and expensive trip halfway across the world to support the Boks. They were easily identifiable in their dark-green Springbok jackets and scarves and beanies – groups of coloured and Indian men mostly. I asked them whether Peter's colour increased their identification with the game. Almost invariably they said yes. They also named the coloured players – Gio Aplon, Juan de Jongh, JP Pietersen – as particular heroes.

So the question is: would showing rugby on free-to-air channels help to popularise the game among more black communities? It is in an attempt to answer this question that, after I've seen Louis von Zeuner, I race uptown to see Imtiaz Patel, the CEO of MultiChoice.

Despite Von Zeuner's SMS, and regular phone calls from me to his PA warning of my late arrival, I'm worried that, now that I have missed my allotted slot with Imtiaz, I might not get to see him at all. This is a man with a lot on his plate.

I've interviewed Imtiaz Patel before and found him

exceptionally sharp. He is a good-looking man in his forties with the wiry grace of the former ace bowler. Born and brought up in the small North West town of Schweizer-Reneke, he qualified initially as a teacher at Wits University. He then taught for four years at a private school in Soweto, where he became involved in cricket development. He rapidly rose in the ranks of the United Cricket Board under Ali Bacher, and it was assumed he would succeed Bacher as CEO. Instead, he was pipped at the post by the now-disgraced Gerald Majola. He joined SuperSport, where he became CEO. Now he heads SuperSport's parent, MultiChoice.

I have a brief wait in a slightly shabby lounge, studiedly casual with charcoal background and brightly coloured cushions, before he comes out to greet me and leads me into a meeting room. He's in the middle of negotiating some big deal. His cellphone buzzes and he says 'Sorry, I have to take this,' briefly leaving the room. When he returns, he is reading out Louis von Zeuner's SMS, which he's only just seen. Quick as a flash, he types back: 'You whiteys are always late!'

I can see that he's harassed, and so I quickly get to the point, which is my contention that free TV would help transform rugby. This is clearly an argument he has heard before and he doesn't hide his irritation with it.

'That is bullshit! Bullshit!

'There is a misperception that, if something is on TV, it becomes more popular. That's number one. There's a misperception that you help transformation by putting it on free TV or e.tv. That black people will then play the sport and you will get a load of black people in the national team. It's a lot of bullshit.

'In 1999, I pioneered a transformation project that lasted eighteen months and resulted in quotas being set at schoolboy level and at provincial level, and only when schoolboys were exposed at that level and had opportunities at that level did it work. Because every provincial team had to have a minimum of five black players. That is the ONLY way you will get players into our national team!

'My second argument is that English Premiership is the most popular league in the world. Manchester United and Arsenal are known in any village in the world. Wayne Rooney is recognised and Manchester United merchandise is worn everywhere. The other day, I went to Schweizer-Reneke, a village in the sticks of the sticks, and there were Man U shirts. If you go anywhere in India or in China, Man United is supported. How? I don't see them on free TV anywhere in the world. So administrators who look for free TV as the panacea for their transformation problems are incompetent. Nothing short of trying to hide behind their incompetence! Because the thing that will drive transformation is a plan, a development programme that is executed properly. And a commitment by coaches at all levels to ensure that transformation actually does happen.'

He's talking rapid-fire at me, not waiting for a response. But, in fact, I wouldn't contest anything he is saying.

'If you argue that you want greater viewership, then let's argue that. Let's not hide transformation behind more viewership. If you want more viewership, you'll get less money. And that's your trade-off. Because paid-for TV pays for sport everywhere in the world. You will then have to decide whether you will go for free TV and sacrifice millions which otherwise could have gone into the development programme, which is really the answer to transforming the sport. So you kill the development programme; you don't transform the sport but you get the viewership.

'I was involved with Ali Bacher in the early 2000s when we were fooled by our own ideals. We thought that, if we wanted to transform sport, we needed to have it on free TV – at the cost of millions. If I look back today, I would rather have had those millions to build stadiums and facilities and had proper coaches whom I could have paid full-time!'

Transformation in cricket has gone into reverse since his time there, he says. In fact, it is in a dire state. 'Why? Cricket is still on free TV. But cricket ratings have gone down. It's less popular than rugby. Fewer than 2 000 people attend a popular local cricket game. You get 40 000 people to a popular rugby game. So the story about free TV being the panacea for everyone's problems is bullshit: ask Irvin Khoza why, in 1997, he did a deal with SuperSport. He renewed it in 2011 for another five years. Where was local football when free TV was their partner? And where is local football now? And I'm not talking Bafana because they are not our partners. I'm talking PSL, which is now ranked in the top ten of world leagues in terms of commercial activities and sponsorship value. Their sponsorship value has more than doubled since they made SuperSport their partner. Income has quadrupled. The quality of the league is ten times better than it used to be.'

The last time I interviewed Patel, he was charming. I've clearly caught him on a bad day. But I'm grateful that he's made time for me and has been relatively open. And one can't fault his logic. SuperSport, together with ABSA, provides more than 80% of SARU's income. But the way it is spent is not up to them.

* * *

Andy Colquhoun, former rugby writer and now SARU's general manager of corporate affairs, is charged with shaping the image of SARU. He is almost too good at his job. Before he took over, there was a scandal a week. Now all the drama goes on behind closed doors and communication is via a stream of press releases. The downside of this rigorous media management is that SARU is increasingly opaque.

I visited their offices one day to see AnneLee Murray who, besides looking after the Bok wives, is responsible for administering the commercial rights of the Springboks. Part of this is ensuring the players wear only the correctly branded clothing. Virtually everything they wear – from mouthguards to underwear – is bespoke. You can't have a pair of underpants sticking out with a subtle yellow stripe, for instance, because it might constitute guerrilla marketing.

'I spend a lot of time keeping the sponsors happy,' she says. 'They've paid a lot for it.' Sponsorship entitles a company to a certain number of team appearances at corporate events, and involving the team in campaigns.

'I coordinate a couple of hundred appearances each year. I make sure the players get to the shoot and that they are wearing the correct gear. It's the Springbok logo that's important. That is what people are paying for. We have a marketing department that makes sure all the logos are correct. I make sure the players are properly briefed. I get Springbok media manager De Jongh Borchardt to write the speech and make sure the player is comfortable with what he is asked to do. Some can make speeches. Others just do question-and-answer sessions.'

Acquiring and maintaining sponsorship can be a tricky business. Everyone wants to be associated with a winning team. The US team at the World Cup found this out to their cost. While the Springboks had every variety of clothing they could possibly need, the Americans, with the same sponsor – Canterbury – got the absolute minimum.

But this lavish provision comes with demands: within the team hotel, for instance, players can wear only the sponsor's clothing, for all those many occasions when someone pops up with a camera.

The Springboks also market themselves individually, but SARU restricts the use of its branding. Players can't use the Springbok emblem, for instance, or wear Springbok colours. And Jean de Villiers can't describe himself in an advert as Springbok captain. He can only refer to himself as an international rugby player.

At the Rugby World Cup, the International Rugby Board has a monopoly on sponsorship. It was not only the tsunami that garnered sympathy for the Samoan team: it was also the perceived unfairness of the IRB, who fined the team NZ$10 000 (almost R60 000) because one of their wings wore a mouthguard displaying one of the Samoan sponsors' branding. The players' teeth, along with the display space on their bodies, were leased out to the IRB. Only the IRB is allowed to make money from sponsorship at the World Cup.

12 Schalk Burger

Watching Schalk Burger at the Samoa game, crashing into one granite-hard body after another, I think of a conversation I had with him earlier in the year, which, I thought, gave me some insight into his inner workings. I asked him how he relaxed and he said: 'I have no problem relaxing. I have a flatscreen TV and a leather couch and I just watch sport – any sport. I'm also addicted to crashes on YouTube. I watch car crashes, plane crashes – any crashes.' So that's how he psyches himself into it.

For several years, Schalk was considered to be the next Springbok captain-elect. He was captain of Super Rugby's 2011 South African conference-winning Stormers, a member of the Bok senior players' group and a man widely respected for leading by example on the field. For all these reasons, I held regular conversations with him in 2011, following the build-up to the Rugby World Cup through his eyes.

I visited his family and, on two occasions, had lengthy chats with his father, also named Schalk. The first time was at Kleinmond, at the family's seaside home. It was 12.30 but Schalk senior and I demolished a bottle of his Sauvignon Blanc. It was so good I've been buying it for home consumption ever since. He is a big man with a voracious grip on life – a book on his own, really. When I left, he gave me a bottle of red wine called Patriot. A label attached to it read: 'Thank you for being a patriot.' I felt honoured at having passed the test.

This first meeting was a getting-to-know-you, off-the-record affair, which I regretted proposing because it was, of course, far more interesting than the subsequent on-the-record conversation at the family's wine estate just outside Wellington. Here I met Myra, Schalk senior's wife, a slim, pretty woman with long, dark hair and her son's wide blue eyes.

What I can report is that our Springbok almost-captain comes with a rich pedigree. He grew up surrounded by musicians and artists. He himself is an accomplished guitarist. His sister is married to the drummer from Prime Circle. Their wine farm, Welbedacht, is a civilised place, producing very good wines in a gorgeous setting. It also contains a cricket pitch and pavilion. Schalk senior has a substantial library on the Anglo-Boer War. His first love was cricket, but his father wouldn't let him play it because it was the colonialists' game. Instead he excelled at rugby, becoming, like his son, a Springbok. Schalk made his money from Megapro, the sports marketing company. I get the sense that toughness is prized in this family.

Schalk junior, funnily enough, also became a Springbok by chance. He was a brilliant cricketer at school, but he got injured playing a rugby game, which ruled him out of selection for the next cricket season. And so he came to concentrate on rugby instead.

All Springboks balance national duty with their provincial commitments. So my conversations with Schalk junior during the build-up to the World Cup are laced with his immediate concern: winning the 2011 Super Rugby Trophy.

Just before the provisional World Cup squad met for their

first two-day training camp at the beginning of May, he told me: 'The hardest competition in the world to win is Tri Nations, because you are playing every week and you are playing the best two sides in the world: Australia and New Zealand. At the World Cup, you get off to an easier start – you are not playing as tough competition. The big thing with the World Cup is how you handle the pressure of the play-offs: those three big games – quarterfinals, semifinals, finals – are two to three times more intense than any other game you have played in your life. So, although you get off to an easy start, play-offs do take bottle; you have to be super-tough to get through them. And Super Rugby is also very tough: it runs through from February to August and it is a very long time to have to stay top of your game. And every week is an important game.'

On 30 April, the Sharks came to Newlands, and this was immediately followed by the first World Cup Springbok camp. A few days before, I chatted with Schalk about it: 'The Springbok camp is on Sunday and Monday at the Newlands Southern Sun. It's the first time we are all getting together this year. It's a big group – not the finalised group, so we will discuss a lot of technical detail. There's not much training we will be able to do because we will all have played the day before and the Sunday and Monday are normally days we take to recover. At the end of the day, our focus is not with the Boks at the moment, although it will be nice seeing all the boys together. We will have played the Sharks the day before so it will be nice if we have won when we rock up there because everyone will be talking about it,' he grins.

'It's fun, hey. Looking forward to it.'

But it does come with sacrifices.

'I'm a bit sad actually – I normally go for a boozy lunch on Sunday, so that's been cancelled. I don't think we'll be having a boozy lunch with the Springbok squad!'

In fact, the Stormers performed brilliantly that Saturday against the Sharks, beating them comprehensively, with a 32-12 final score. Schalk limped off in the second half with a calf strain, ceding the captaincy to Jean de Villiers, who was himself newly back from a lay-off due to ankle injury. Afterwards declared man of the match, De Villiers was at his mercurial, deft-witted best, leading the Stormers in a sparkling attacking game to four tries and a bonus point, and second-highest position on the overall Super 15 log, just behind the Bulls.

As I watch Schalk put in his usual passionate, half-crazed performance until his body rebels, in the form of that temporarily debilitating calf injury, I wonder what internal mechanism he has to tap into to get there. It takes great courage, of course, but also an abandonment to the moment, whatever the consequences. He has already been off for four weeks with an injury this year; the way he plays – with total disregard for any bodily vulnerability – invites further injury. Further injury might rule him out of the World Cup, which, whatever he might say now, must be the pinnacle of his dreams. It will be his third.

A couple of days later, back at the High Performance Centre, I try to get him to explain this to me. He thinks for a bit, intense blue eyes trained on me, and then answers in the third person: 'It was a massive performance: no one really know why. But the biggest challenge about that performance is to produce the same performance again this week [against the Crusaders]. You play your match of the season one week and, seven days later, you've probably got to play better because it's a bigger challenge. We had a chat about it. But what we've lost since then – the guys are a bit sore and energy levels are a bit low after last week – we gain in confidence which we take from the performances.'

Talk me through your position, I say. What exactly does an openside flank do?

'We defend vacuums. We try to slow the ball down on defence. We all do it a bit differently. I'm a bit bigger and I've got a bigger physical aspect than Heinrich Brüssow or George Smith. I'm probably not as good as them on the ground but I probably make up for it in physicality. But it's the basics: you've got to work pretty hard and make plenty of tackles and, when you do get the ball in hand, you've got to have fun with it – either pass it or run with it or try to chip-kick, although I'm not very good at that.

'But, a lot of times, loose forwards especially set up the trend of the game. They can make a big hit early on in the game with turnover and put the team on its way. Every loose forward in this competition has a massive contribution – unlike being wing, for example, or fullback, where you do important stuff but you're not making 80 contributions in 80 minutes. You're making 20 contributions but every one of them is important. What's important for a loose forward is a high work rate, and if you can couple that with intensity and accuracy you are a very good player.'

Off the field, Burger glazes his quivering physical intensity with a layer of languidness, as if he is playing at being laid-back. With his mane of bright blond hair and watchful gaze, he reminds me of a big cat, temporarily at rest. This image carries through from the field: when he is tackling, he can look like a lion bringing down a hapless buck.

I put this to him and he smiles and says: 'I don't know. I'm just trying to stop them as quickly as possible. The Sharks have got big ball-carriers, so I was basically just trying to get hold of them as quickly as I could and wrestle them to the ground. There wasn't much technique involved, but probably a lot of force. It wasn't a conscious decision: it just happens when I'm tired and getting a bit worked up.'

The following weekend, the Stormers take on the Crusaders. As Schalk puts it when I catch up with him again at the High Performance Centre: 'It is the Crusaders who are the trendsetters; they've got the superstars, so, if you want to be the best, you've got to produce against a quality side. So, if we just rock up this weekend and go through the motions, we're going to lose, but, if we play really well, we might lose but we will give ourselves a shot at winning. Last year, we were in a similar situation and we rocked up with a good performance against them and we're looking to do the same again this week.'

What he – and the rest of South Africa – hadn't bargained for was the rapturous welcome the New Zealand team got from a sizeable selection of what they had assumed to be their faithful supporters at Newlands. The welcome was for one superstar in particular: centre Sonny Bill Williams. Newly converted to Islam and part Samoan, he speaks to many Capetonians still embittered by their exclusion from the game during apartheid – solely on the grounds that their skin colour resembled that of Williams. It mostly came from middle-aged people who, like Peter de Villiers and Stormers coach Allister Coetzee, were told as children that they would never be allowed to wear the national jersey because it was only for whites. No doubt their anger is amplified and sustained by a sense of larger, ongoing marginalisation, because, even under the new democracy, they feel they are neither white enough nor black enough.

We watch in dismay as the Stormers are booed by fellow Capetonians as they get off the bus, and then have to listen to rapturous applause for the Kiwis throughout the game. Whether or not this dispiriting atmosphere was a contributing factor, the Stormers went down 20-14, despite the fact that the Crusaders were playing without six of their stars, including Richie McCaw, Dan Carter and Israel Dagg.

On 7 June 2011, just after the next Springbok World Cup camp, I chat to Schalk again: 'We got together – the second time we've been together as a Bok group – reduced from 50 players to 37. Our previous meeting was more about rugby principles. It was more rugby-specific this weekend. Rassie is heading up the technical side with the incumbent coaches, Dick Muir and Gary Gold, Percy and Peter. We got all our calls through, the way we want to play. The way forward: trying to sort out our kicking game. It is always a bit awkward so early on because the team hasn't been selected and it is pretty difficult to give input. It is the Super Rugby climax now, so – I was giving some input there but my mind was still doing Super Rugby – once [that] is finished and everyone has done their bit there I think it will come a lot more naturally than this weekend. We spent Sunday there and Monday there [at the Springbok camp]. We travelled back Monday night and landed at 7pm in Cape Town. Went straight into the planning for the Cheetahs on Tuesday morning early.

'So it's been a hectic couple of weeks since we've been back. It's always like that. You spend a month overseas, no one phones you, no one wants to see you and, in Australia especially, hardly anyone recognises you, so it's fantastic for us just to go out and have some fun, but then you get a double whammy when you get back to South Africa – besides seeing family and friends, you've got sponsor requirements and functions and golf days, so I'm a bit short on sleep, but, once I hit Bloem on Friday, I'll have an early night.'

How are you feeling?

'At this stage of the season, for us, it's pretty taxing on the body. But at least there's big incentive: it's not like we're in the competition but we can't achieve anything. We've got a determined group of players and the boys have been managing their bodies well enough. This weekend we need a win against the Cheetahs to get a bye weekend which is actually a bit of a bonus and a home semifinal.'

They beat the Cheetahs 44-34 and got their bye – and their home semifinal. On 2 July, they faced the Crusaders at Newlands and lost again, 10-29. On 1 September, along with the rest of the team, Schalk boarded the flight to New Zealand, home of the Crusaders.

13 The Big Bok Loss

The fateful quarterfinal against Australia is on 9 October at the Wellington stadium. At 6pm, we kick off into a mild, wind-free evening. We win the line-out. Schalk Burger gets the ball but loses it. Radike Samo picks it up and passes to Wallaby captain James Horwill, who crashes over for a try. It is the 11th minute and this is to be the only try of the game. James O'Connor lines up for the conversion. And misses. Six minutes later, the Wallabies force a penalty, which O'Connor does succeed in kicking over. The Wallabies are up 8-0.

In the 20th minute, disaster strikes. Heinrich Brüssow goes off with a rib injury and is replaced by Francois Louw. Brüssow is crucial to countering David Pocock in the breakdown, which referee Bryce Lawrence appears to have declared a free-for-all. In the 39th minute, we finally get three points on the board, courtesy of a penalty kick by Morné Steyn. On half-time, he tries for another, this time from 60m. He misses. A silent cry issues from South African lips: the other Steyn would have got it in! The half-time score sticks at a miserable 8-3.

Shortly into the second half, Jean de Villiers, back in the starting line-up in the number 12 jersey, passes to Pat Lambie, who dives over the line. A try! No, says Bryce Lawrence, it was a forward pass. The score is still 8-3 to the Australians. The tension is unbearable. For the first time, I begin to think we're not going to make it. In the 50th minute, Peter de

Villiers finally replaces John Smit with Bismarck du Plessis. Habana also goes off and Francois Hougaard runs on. Six minutes later, Morné Steyn kicks over another penalty. We're in the lead! 9-8. We're dominating territory and possession but we just can't push through to a try. Then Fourie du Preez wins the ball from a scrum close to the Wallaby tryline. He is tackled by two Wallabies and loses it. Pat Lambie picks it up and kicks for the poles. He misses, but only just. Poor Pat. Two near hits, either of which would have made him a national hero at the ripe old age of twenty. First the disallowed try and now the wayward drop goal.

And then, the final blow: an assistant referee tells Bryce Lawrence that Danie Rossouw has knocked Radike Samo's legs out from under him as he jumped for the ball in a line-out. Lawrence awards the Wallabies a penalty. All 40 000-odd spectators hold their breath as O'Connor prepares to kick. It's over. In the remaining ten minutes, we fail to score again. At full time, the score is 11-9 to Australia.

Our World Cup is over.

At the media conference afterwards, John Smit and Peter de Villiers are too stunned for sophistry. These are the two men who have been consistently blamed for the Boks' tribulations. A decent showing at the World Cup would have meant vindication. All chance of that has now gone.

De Villiers doesn't hide his devastation. Asked to describe his mood, he responds: 'Three notches lower than a funeral.'

Smit has three raw red gashes down his right cheek. He launches into a paean of praise for Peter: 'As much pain as we're going through now, Peter has given us leeway and space. It's sad to end it like this.'

The stats show that South Africa had 56% of possession and 76% of territory. We won all our own scrums and stole five of the Wallabies' line-outs. The Aussies were forced to make 147 tackles, compared with our 53, and they conceded two more penalties than we did. But all that counts is the numbers up on the scoreboard. They won. We lost.

Back in the media centre, I have a drink with my colleagues, knowing it will be the last. I watch while they churn out copy, detailing every last miserable minute for the public back home, in the full knowledge that they probably won't want to read it. This is the end of the road for all of us, too. Several of them will be on the first flight home.

I get onto the media shuttle to Ekhaya, the South African government's hospitality centre at the Amora, the Springboks' current hotel, in downtown Wellington. All the brass are there, sitting at individual tables, too morose for company. Sports Minister Fikile Mbalula, nursing a glass of white wine, says his staff had wanted him to delay his visit till the semis, but something had told him he had to come now. He's full of sympathy for the boys. There is no judgement. Regan Hoskins, Mark Alexander and Jurie Roux, respectively president, vice-president and CEO of SARU, hover, disconsolate. No one expected this. I commiserate and then head off to Courtney Place, Wellington's party precinct, which is wild with Aussie delight. The Welsh are there, too, still celebrating their win against Ireland the night before. In Nando's, I find several clumps of South Africans, comfort-eating home food. They are too depressed to say much except: what the hell do we do here now?

It is even worse the following week in Auckland: the rain

beats down day after day and I keep bumping into damp green-clad men who have flown over specifically for the semifinal, so confident that we would be in it. New Zealand is expensive for South Africans, and these guys had paid World Cup-inflated prices for accommodation and flights. The six-week trip to New Zealand had set me back almost R100 000, and I didn't have to pay for tickets to the games, as these guys did.

Still trying to come to terms with it all, I read the local papers to get their take: the most opinionated commentary is from a Kiwi writer, Gregor Paul. He sees the early ejection of England and South Africa as evidence of a new order in world rugby. 'Rugby could be on the verge of a renaissance now that creativity and enterprise have emerged as the key World Cup characteristics. All those fears that defence and kicking would reign supreme as they did four years ago have proven unfounded. Rugby is dancing to a new beat. Pass and catch has taken off – it is the new bible of world rugby. Those who didn't embrace it have gone home. It would have been a travesty had England progressed beyond the quarterfinals – they just weren't a team on whom the game could be grown. Their basic skills were poor and rugby would have been dragged back to the Dark Ages had they won.

'South Africa paid a similar price. Maybe a lenient referee didn't help their cause at the breakdown but, when they come to review how it was they had so much possession and didn't score against Australia, all roads will lead back to their lack of manipulation and inability to exploit space.'

Imagine rugby, concludes Paul, 'that is as elegant as it is feral'. 'Wales, France, Australia and New Zealand – they are the choice of the romantic. These four can show that skill, pace and adventure can triumph.'

So, was it our conservative style of rugby and inability to adapt that defeated us, as it did the English? If so, who is to blame? The players, who resisted Peter de Villiers's early attempts to change their game? SARU, who appointed De Villiers and then undermined him so that he was driven to form an alliance with the senior players, with them at the helm? Whatever, I decide to pack my bags and go home. Without the Springboks there to give my days structure and purpose, it feels meaningless. I don't care who wins now.

* * *

Once home, I am bemused by the lack of introspection. England, who fared exactly as we did – falling out at the quarterfinals – are subjected to a flailing. Boards of inquiry are appointed. Martin Johnson, the head coach, immediately falls on his sword and resigns.

We blame Bryce Lawrence. And quietly move on. The entire management team's four-year contracts lapse at the end of December 2011. On 27 January 2012, Heyneke Meyer is announced as the new head coach. The general feeling seems to be that he should have got it last time round, instead of Peter de Villiers. The clock has simply been wound back, the past four years wiped out.

I ask Mike Greenaway, veteran rugby writer for the *Daily News* and ghost writer of John Smit's autobiography, *Captain in the Cauldron*, to tell the game as he saw it: 'At the beginning of the game there was a feeling that the stars were not in line for us. The ball was going to bounce wrong. Sometimes that just happens in sport. It's one of the vagaries.

'For instance, that try scored by James Horwill. The Wallabies had been defending the whole game so far and they had a rare foray into the Boks' 22. We had won the line-out. We were driving it up to try to get a bit of space to clear it. There's a ruck. It bounces off a shin into an Aussie lock's hands and, in the context of the game, it was a ridiculously soft try. But that is one of the differences between winning and losing. Just a freakish soft try.

'And then the poor old Boks – freakish things happening like Fourie du Preez going for the line, having his elbow tapped and the ball spinning forward. A fantastic build-up to what would have been a try by Pat Lambie, but a forward pass right at the end of about fifteen very good phases.

'There were things early in the game when Heinrich Brüssow was harshly taken out by one of the Aussies, and maybe that was preconceived, knowing what losing a guy like Brüssow could do to us in a game where the ref wasn't blowing the breakdown and players like Brüssow and Pocock could really climb in. As Pocock did. And then you didn't have Brüssow there to counter him. So that was another big factor.

'The big talking point about that game was the failure of Bryce to officiate at the breakdown. He just didn't take charge. When the Boks were defeated, that was the thing seized upon by the South African public and, with there being a ready-made scapegoat in the form of the referee, the Boks were saved from being crucified for what was ultimately quite a failure – to go out at the quarterfinals.

'Given the Boks' World Cup record, that is really bad. So,

of course, they would rather that they had gone further and not had a referee to blame but, as it is, Bryce saved their blushes. And it probably also saved Danie Rossouw from being heavily criticised. That game was so tight. There was so little in it despite the Boks' dominating it, and you can imagine the leaders on both sides were saying: "Guys, whatever we do, let's keep our discipline. Discipline is key here. We cannot give away penalties." And then we have one of our players committing a silly offence at a line-out, which they are nailed for. O'Connor kicks the penalty and they win. But it's all Bryce Lawrence's fault!'

An insider told me that the plan had been to start Bismarck at the quarterfinals, with Victor as captain and John on the bench. But Smit had put pressure on De Villiers to start him and De Villiers had given in. 'Smit was a great captain,' said the source, 'but, at the World Cup, he lost it.'

As October comes to an end, there is a temporary distraction: the 2011 Currie Cup is reaching its own climax. The returning Boks slot straight back in, relieved to be back on the field. Playing in the Currie Cup semifinal is not quite the same as the World Cup semifinal, but it's better than sitting at home licking your wounds.

Just before Schalk Burger went up to Joburg to take on the Lions at Ellis Park in the semifinal, I had a chat with him. I'm treading carefully because I know how raw and painful the subject is but I would like to hear what he thinks.

'We always knew that Wales was going to be tough and then Fiji and Samoa would also be difficult because they are so big and because of the abrasive way they play. There was a lot of feeling in the Samoa match because for them it was make or break, and we knew that they were going to fire up and there was a fair bit of niggle on the field and off the field there were quite a few chirps, but we got through it. So we got the job done. And then fortunately for us we played one of our better games in the quarterfinal – for the World Cup and for the past year, I suppose. But unfortunately – the result didn't go our way.'

Does he blame Bryce Lawrence, I ask.

'You never know,' he responds. 'Sometimes I suppose it's timing. In the previous World Cup, we were probably lucky. We peaked at the right time – it was our time and we managed to win it comfortably. For this World Cup, we had a similar feeling, that we were peaking at the right time. We were playing a good brand of rugby, and even in the quarterfinals there was a belief we were going to win it. But unfortunately, it wasn't our time. Maybe through some bad decisions, maybe through some bad luck. It wasn't our time, and I don't think we can argue much better than that. We can go on about the ref's decisions and players' mistakes and we can discuss that till we are eighty or ninety or till we die. And, much as it hurts, the fact of the matter is that we fell out in the quarterfinals.'

As usual with Schalk, he carries physical as well as emotional scars: 'In the Namibia game, I got a cut in the head and had it stitched up. And then again in the quarterfinal. It's never fun getting stitched up and going out there again, but adrenaline is the most powerful drug in the world and we were all fired up. If it was a lesser match – like a Currie Cup match – I would not be too happy, but being a World Cup, only once in every four years, I just get it stitched it up quickly and get out there again and play some more rugby.'

Despite the bitter ending, he enjoyed the 2011 World Cup, he says. And the one before that. 'My first one was under very difficult circumstances, but they are always fun to be around; it's just a pity we didn't go further in the competition. But, again, there are some big players hanging up their boots, and being part of that Springbok side for the past eight years has been phenomenal, and I think every one of us has enjoyed the journey.'

The denouement was particularly brutal, though.

'It changes pretty quickly. Before the game, you don't think about losing. We got back to the hotel probably at around 10.30pm and we had a little meeting there saying goodbye to a few guys. It was quite a sad occasion. Then at 1am we had to have our bags in the truck, and at a quarter to four we were picked up by our bus, and early the next day we arrived back in South Africa, so, when it's over, it's over suddenly. There is no drawing back and thinking about it.

'You hurt and you are a bit depressed but somehow you are going to get over it. This weekend, we have a different challenge, which is nice. It takes the mind off the fact that we failed at the World Cup.

'We can't redeem what happened at the World Cup, but life goes on, and maybe this year is our time for Western Province. Because me and a couple of my mates have been here for ages and we've had some fantastic seasons – especially in the last three years, we've given ourselves a lot of chances but we haven't been able to get our hands on a piece of silverware, but maybe this time. It is about timing, and maybe this time Lady Luck is on our side.'

Unfortunately, though, it ended in another loss – for all

the Boks. The Lions, virtually Springbok-free and therefore able to achieve team cohesion over the four months of the Currie Cup campaign, won the Cup, defeating first Western Province and then the Sharks.

For Schalk Burger, 2011 at least ended well. He was crowned Player of the Year. But in 2012, the fates again turn on him. An anterior cruciate ligament injury in his first game of the year keeps him off the field for the rest of the year, despite two bouts of surgery. At the beginning of 2013, he makes a starry appearance at the Stormers' training camp in Hermanus, bright blond hair standing up like a halo above those wide blue eyes. Allister Coetzee proudly announces him as restored to the Stormers' captaincy, giving Jean de Villiers a much-welcomed break. As Coetzee speaks, Burger's chair collapses under him. It proves to be auspicious. His return to the field is delayed by a new injury, this time to his calf. The knee is fine but, for some reason, he just can't sprint. After yet another operation – this time to drain a cyst on his spine, which is affecting a nerve in his leg – this hulk of a man is felled by another blow: bacterial meningitis.

During his convalescence, he stands on the edge of the field, watching his team play on without him. He looks thinner and uncharacteristically subdued. This enforced inactivity is very frustrating. 'I'm missing it, hey!' he says. But it will be several months at best before he is back in the game.

14 The Owners

In April 2013, I went to SARU's AGM at the Southern Sun hotel in Newlands. This is the annual meeting of rugby's most powerful body, the General Council, made up of the 14 unions who own South African rugby. There are 28 men seated around three sides of a long rectangular table. Each union, no matter what its size, has two votes. So two men sit behind each of the 14 signs indicating the union they represent. At the top is the 13-strong executive council whom they elect, largely from their own ranks, to carry out their commands. I've waited a year to see this, as it is the only SARU gathering that the media is allowed to attend. The agenda is brief but weighty: the AGM is required to approve the 2012 annual statement audited by PricewaterhouseCoopers, whose team sit at the back, available for questions. The annual budget is a hefty R688 million.

There are about fifty people in the room and I am the only woman. This – and the fact that eight of the union presidents are white, five are coloured and only one is African – gives the impression of an organisation that has not kept up with the times. Frequent references are made to the fact that 'the media is present'. In other words, be careful what you say. In fact, the only media present are me and Stephen Nell from *Rapport*. This is a dramatic contrast to the legions of media who gather to judge the performance of players and coaches. This, the font of power in rugby, goes largely unscrutinised.

The glossy annual reports we are handed show the names of the presidents popping up also in the various SARU subcommittees: Audit and Risk, Finance, Games and Policies, Elite Player Development, Development and Transformation, Constitutional.

Andre May, the president of the Leopards, one of the smaller unions, raises his hand: he wants more money. This is the gist of it, although the way it is couched is this: each of the 14 unions gets an annual hand-out of R7.4 million from broadcasting rights. The unions that have Super Rugby franchises – the Bulls, the Stormers, the Sharks, the Cheetahs, the Lions and, this year at least, the Southern Kings – each get an additional R6.6 million. Andre May wants this second sum to be split between all 14 unions. The current split was hammered out years ago, before the last round of Sanzar talks on a new broadcast agreement effective from 2011 to 2015. So trying to get this changed on the hoof seems, at the very least, time-wasting and mischievous.

After some to-ing and fro-ing, the emollient SARU president, Oregan Hoskins, who is chairing, succeeds in getting the matter deferred to yet another meeting.

The final items on the agenda are the approval of fees for the auditors and a 7% pay rise for the executive council.

At this point, Hein Mentz, the president of another of the minnows, the Mpumalanga Rugby Union, raises his hand. He is not prepared to agree to the 7% raise until he knows what the members of the executive council are being paid. Under SARU's constitution, this man is an owner and has been for many years. Surely he has this information? Besides which, in the audited financial statements in front of him, there is a section headed: 'Executive Council Members' Remuneration'. The total is close on R10 million. Divide that by the number of men sitting at the top table and you'd get a ballpark figure.

After more fruitless exchanges, Hoskins succeeds in getting this issue, too, postponed to another meeting.

I'm not sure whether postponement is a tactic to avoid confronting issues or whether they want to discuss these in closed meetings. Both these interventions seem mystifyingly petty and obstructive to me until I understand that there is an underlying agenda: at next year's AGM, the executive council positions come up for re-election. This is probably all about jostling for position and sounding out potential alliances. Looking for a bigger slice of the pie.

After the meeting is over, I ask SARU chief financial officer Basil Haddad to explain the 2012 SARU budget to me. The gist of it is that, out of total income of R688 845 101, fully R272 315 371, or more than 39%, comes from sponsorship. Broadcasting rights bring in R307 140 378, or 44%. In other words, by far the largest contributors to SARU funds are SuperSport and the other sponsors, chief among them ABSA. On the operations side, the total budget stands at R697 604 796, with the lion's share claimed by the Commercial and Marketing category, at R231 593 599 (33.1% of the total). Haddad explains that this category includes the holding of Test matches. The High Performance category (R149 269 660, or 21%) goes mainly to the Sevens and the Springboks, but also covers the Junior Boks and the Women's team. The Springboks on their own cost SARU 'between R60 million and R70 million'. That includes salaries, travel and training camps. The Development budget (R68 478 559, or 9.8%)

includes all the amateur activities, including Craven Week and Coca-Cola Week and the new Cell C Community Cup. It also funds development programmes, which are entrusted to the various unions. A handful of the struggling unions owe SARU just under R25 million in loans. This is in addition to the R140 million shared out between them.

I'm surprised by the fact that, although our national team attracts the most income – through broadcasting and sponsors – they are awarded only around 10% of SARU's annual budget. The Springboks are also paid by their franchises, of course, so some of the additional funds paid to the big unions also go to Springboks.

The men sitting around the table are mostly ex-players, with the odd accountant, doctor and lawyer. Some of them are big fish in very small ponds, but they are astute enough in finding ways to hang onto power. SARU's structural underpinning, despite the mighty edifice it sustains, is as flimsy as that of a local amateur club. SARU's official description is: 'an incorporated association of persons with perpetual succession and juristic personality'. It is not even what was known under the old Companies Act as a Section 21 company, like Cricket South Africa. To meet sponsor requirements, they provide a professionally audited financial statement. But this is voluntary. They follow the Companies Act and King III where they feel it is appropriate. In other words, they are a law unto themselves. Both Hein Mentz and Andre May sit on the SARU constitutional subcommittee.

The General Council is astute enough to choose a personable and dynamic CEO as its public face. But even Jurie Roux seems to battle with some of the men he works for.

I leave the AGM with the following conclusion: that there is both good and bad here. It's wrong to lump all rugby administrators together as a problem – which is a fairly common perspective. Virtually everyone I have spoken to in rugby sees the make-up of SARU as deeply problematic. Reform is difficult because it would require a voluntary renunciation of power and privilege. 'You wouldn't get a turkey to vote for Christmas!' is the sentence I often hear.

But SARU needs to lift its game. It needs to be as ruthless as the Springbok coach has to be about dropping non-performers who drag the team down. It's clear who these are: the minnow unions that suck energy from meetings like this and funding from the rugby fiscus, which would be much better spent elsewhere.

For the first time in its history, SARU has carried out a survey that shows how many schools and clubs play rugby in the areas controlled by each of its 14 constituent unions and, in its 2012 annual report, promised that the results would be available by March 2013. Repeated requests for this have been stonewalled, presumably because SARU does not want it to be known just how tiny is the number of players presided over by some of its member unions. But another, broader survey presented to Parliament by Jurie Roux early in 2012 gives a fairly clear idea, even though the areas described are 'geo-political provincial unions', rather than SARU ones.

Anyone watching the 2013 Vodacom Cup would notice how the team fielded by the Pumas was overwhelmingly white, and how even the beautiful Mbombela Stadium in which they played their home games failed to attract more than a handful of fans. The SARU survey is revealing:

a minuscule 3% of schools and clubs in Mpumalanga play rugby. There is no justification for the coterie of men who make up this union to wield power over the national team or to drain money away from it. And the same goes for other small unions.

Surely it is wrong that the Mpumalanga Rugby Union, representing such a tiny proportion of the country's rugby players, should have exactly the same voting power over the national game as the giants, such as the Sharks, Western Province and the Blue Bulls?

The reason for the ridiculous amount of power still vested in these minnow unions is that SARU is still rooted in the distant era of amateur rugby. Perhaps it was because of our long isolation from international rugby that our administration has failed to keep up with developments elsewhere in the world. It is now more then two decades since the last major reform in rugby, the 1996 intervention by Louis Luyt, which saw the ruthless but necessary pruning of the number of unions from 23 to 14. Another such cull is long overdue.

What I'd recommend is that the General Council be streamlined, with the bottom six unions absorbed into the top eight unions.

Also in urgent need of modernisation is the executive council, previously known as the board, the executive arm of SARU. At the moment, it comprises the president, vice president, the CEO, CFO, a players' representative, the company secretary, four former union presidents and a couple of co-opted members. In sharp contrast to the General Council, which is largely white, the exco has a predominance of darker faces. This is the more visible body: it is difficult to dismiss a suspicion of window-dressing. And the ex-presidents who take up four of the places on the exco impress more with their tenacity and accumulated age than with their level of skill. This is another SARU team that urgently needs to lift its game.

The current make-up of the General Council and its exco is based on the amateur era, when provincial unions got most of their money from gate takings at their local stadia. Broadcast money has changed all that. Now people watch rugby on SuperSport. Apart from Newlands, more recently the Nelson Mandela Bay Stadium in PE and, some of the time, Kings Park, stadia around the country are more than half-empty, even for Super Rugby games. Few of these facilities are run profitably. Men who have been in rugby administration for the past 20 years, with little leadership or governance experience outside of it, continue to elect each other to the exco.

Hundreds of millions of rands now pour into the SARU head office. The same administrators who handled the small change of the amateur era now are required to administer multi-million-rand budgets. How does an individual with such limited experience manage? An organisation of this size, operating in a highly competitive global arena, needs sophisticated skills in finance, contracting and negotiating.

There was a moment of irony in the middle of the AGM that cast a brief, unflattering spotlight on SARU: Oregan Hoskins announced that the Southern Kings had just drawn with the log-topping Brumbies, playing at the latter's home ground of Canberra – an extraordinary achievement. The Brumbies' fortunes have soared since South African export

Jake White took over as head coach. Just over a year ago, this same General Council announced the Kings' entry into Super Rugby without having worked out how they would make this happen. The consequence was almost a year of dithering, which ended with the Kings getting the green light only a few months before the 2013 season began and the Lions being dumped, despite SARU's initial promise that no existing franchise would be affected by the inclusion of the Kings. SARU tried fruitlessly to persuade Sanzar to add a sixteenth franchise to the Super Rugby structure. (Sanzar, the partnership between South Africa, New Zealand and Australia brought into existence by the 1996 broadcast deal with News Corporation, administers Super Rugby and the Rugby Championship, formerly called the Tri Nations.)

South Africa does not get a good deal from Sanzar, and I believe this is in part due to the fact that SARU does not bring the same negotiating skills to the table. We have the same voting rights as New Zealand and Australia, despite the fact that South Africans make up 62% of viewers, with New Zealanders 26% and Australians 12%. New Zealand and Australia tend to vote as a bloc, outnumbering South Africa.

For the Sanzar negotiations at which the current, five-year broadcast deal was worked out, SARU sent three exco members. They were, no doubt, all decent men who did their best, but they found themselves heavily outclassed by the New Zealanders and Australians, who each came to the table with a dozen highly skilled negotiators. The result was a new, impossible burden for the Springboks. The Super Rugby tournament was extended from May until August with, worst of all, the addition of double-headed local derbies.

The impact of this is only too clear. It is why Heyneke Meyer is landed with a selection of tired players, crippled by injuries. It is also one of the reasons we are seeing the current exodus of star players to Japan: there they won't have their careers shortened by the attrition wrought by endless Super Rugby.

The other reason players leave is that they feel they aren't paid enough. SARU says they simply can't compete with the yen and the euro. There is obviously some truth in this, but there are other factors at play. One is the way SARU has structured its payments: in order for a top Bok to earn around R2 million a year, he has to play in virtually every international game, and the team has to win. Playing in France or Japan guarantees an income at least twice that, without the performance element. So, a player who has set outgoings – bonds, pension and insurance payments – has the security of knowing his monthly direct debits will be met, and that he is building up a lump sum from which to launch a post-rugby career.

Jean de Villiers once made the point to me that we are still in the experimental phases of professional rugby. Like him, most of today's top players were contracted straight from school. If they retire at the age of 35, they will have subjected their bodies to the rigours of the game for 17-odd years. We don't yet know, he said, what the consequence of several surgeries, lacerations and other injuries will have in the long term. Will they be needing to have hip and knee replacements at the age of 40? And, if so, who will pay? If, like Joost van der Westhuizen and Tinus Linee, they fall prey to deadly diseases, will they too have to rely on charity?

South African rugby administrators do little to help players prepare for life, post-rugby. The issue of what happens to Springboks once they are no longer useful to the game comes up with increasing urgency as the era of professional rugby lengthens. Several have now been spewed out of the system in their mid-thirties or earlier. A tiny minority – like Bob Skinstad and Ashwin Willemse – make it as SuperSport commentators. John Smit and Victor Matfield have been lucky enough to be absorbed into management positions at their former unions. A handful of others, such as Jannie and Bismarck du Plessis, have gained professional qualifications while playing. Some have invested wisely and can build on business enterprises started while still in the game. But many more end up with nothing. Recruited by provincial unions straight from school, they bypass the tertiary educational institutions and end up with only a matric to their name. They have little knowledge about how the world works, because they have been in the rugby bubble for fifteen years, with everything done for them: their logistics are taken care of, their diaries plotted out, their cars and boots sponsored. But, the day they hang up their boots, it all comes to an end. Unlike some of the administrators, who contrive to hang onto their positions for decades. Once players have outlived their usefulness on the field, they are discarded.

SARU currently allocates 10% of its overall income to the Springboks – and that includes salaries, travel and training camps. I think they should have another look at their budget and try to find more money for their star team. Around R45 million would become available, for instance, if the six minnow unions were absorbed into the high-functioning unions.

Another R38 million – a sum revealed in the 2011 financial report – could be saved if SARU's exco contained members with the skills to negotiate with sponsors and broadcasters instead of paying this amount in commission to others.

Players elsewhere do better than ours: in the United States, where American football is comparable to rugby here in terms of national prestige and player attrition, the National Football League (NFL) diverts 48% of all its income to player salaries.

The bottom line of all this is, like everything else to do with the national team, stark and visible to anyone who wants to see it: we are not performing as well as we should. And this is largely because the national team has outgrown its owners, who have become a drag on the team.

So, how to fix this? It is worth looking at best practice in other countries and other sporting codes. A good place to start would be the current rugby world champions. The New Zealand Rugby Union General Meeting – its equivalent of our General Council – allocates votes to member unions based on the number of teams each is responsible for. Thus a union with fewer than sixty affiliated teams (which includes high school teams) gets two votes. The number of votes per union graduates upwards to seven votes for unions with 225 or more affiliates. The mercurial rugby New Zealand plays – both skilled and adventurous – reflects the agility of its administrative structures.

The Australian Rugby Union (ARU) has a similar system,

but they have taken it a step further. In 2012, the Minister for Sport, Kate Lundy, ordered a review of the ARU to ascertain whether its governance model reflected modern business practices. Led by Mark Arbib, a former federal sports minister, what became known as the Arbib Review was published in August 2012. It found that while the existing system, clogged with ex-players and the odd accountant, made sense in the amateur era, it did not do so in the professional era. Much like ours, then.

Arbib recommended that the ARU board be composed entirely of independent directors with the right mix of skills and experience. Conflicts of interest had to be removed and accountability to shareholders ensured, as well as transparency in all dealings. Endorsing Arbib, Minister Lundy pointed out that 'a modern governance structure is a prerequisite to support a sustainable and prosperous sporting organization'. The Arbib Review will now lay the foundation for rugby union growth in Australia.

Our own Sports Minister, Fikile Mbalula, has initiated a major shake-up in the administration of sports. Already, he has tackled maladministration in soccer, boxing, athletics and cricket. The most significant for South African rugby – because it is the sport with a comparable history – is cricket. In 2012, Mbalula asked Judge Chris Nicholson to investigate the awarding of suspicious bonuses to Cricket South Africa (CSA) president Gerald Majola, and to look into the administration of the CSA. Nicholson produced an excellent report, not only pinpointing the inadequacies of CSA but also suggesting how they should be remedied in line with international best practice. Like Arbib, he recommended a board of independent directors equipped with appropriate skills. He also found that CSA was failing to develop cricket at grassroots level – like rugby, cricketers come from private schools and former model C schools – even though it was on this basis that it held its tax-exempt Section 21 status. He recommended SARS should investigate this and enforce compliance. SARU, which does pay tax and is not a Section 21 company, is not therefore subject to the same pressures. But it would do well to take note of what is happening in cricket.

The Nicholson report has opened up burning issues in the governance of sport in South Africa. Corporates like ABSA, the Springboks' chief sponsor, need to know that rugby is properly run and that its millions are well used. Unlike SARU, ABSA has to answer to demanding shareholders. Like any other business in South Africa, it also needs to look at the country's demographics for growth – in other words, to black people. And, if SARU cannot justify the millions invested in it with an alignment to the ABSA brand, it might lose that money.

Already, CSA sponsors are taking Nicholson on board. Momentum Life, the chief sponsor, has included a clause in its contract with CSA stipulating that Nicholson's recommendations be enforced.

The SARU executive council needs to follow international best practice and take on a majority of independent directors with the appropriate skills. There is the sudden availability on the market of some former CEOs with the magical combination of the requisite skills, a passion for rugby and a philanthropic desire to give back. Louis von

Zeuner is one of these. Paul Harris, former CEO of FirstRand, is another. Both Harris and Von Zeuner have been involved in the restructuring of CSA. Jacko Maree from Standard Bank will also now have more time on his hands, following his retirement. These men have the trust and respect of corporate South Africa. They are highly experienced in the management of transformation and development in the peculiarly South African context. They know how to get the best from high-performance teams and they have been at the cutting edge of modern governance practices. Also, they are wealthy men who do not need salaries from SARU. They would be truly independent.

But the initiative will have to come from government. Sports Minister Fikile Mbalula has shown an admirable decisiveness in taking on malfunctioning administrations. Hopefully, the reform of rugby will be his next project.

✶ ✶ ✶

One thing most South Africans agree on is that Nelson Mandela represents the best of us. In rugby, of all sports, he has made his expectations clear. It should be a catalyst for transcending bigotry and self-interest and prioritising the greater good. In my tour of the Springbok factory, it has been heartening to see the extent to which this remains a guiding spirit. In homes, schools and teams, I've seen not only the fuzzy, feel-good stuff, but also the striving for excellence. In 2015, two decades after Mandela lifted the Webb Ellis Cup on behalf of his country, our team will make another bid to bring it home. As long as the blokes in the boardroom play ball, there is no reason why they shouldn't.

Crunching the numbers

Springbok all-time records

	Played	Won	Lost	Drawn	Win %
Total	413	259	133	21	62.7
Home	221	151	57	13	68.3
Away (includes neutral venues)	192	108	76	8	56.3

Against New Zealand

	Played	Won	Lost	Drawn	Win %
	85	34	48	3	40.0

Against Australia

	Played	Won	Lost	Drawn	Win %
	76	42	33	1	55.3

In Tri Nations (Rugby Championship)

	Played	Won	Lost	Drawn	Win %
Total	72	28	43	1	38.9
Home	36	22	14	0	61.1
Away	36	6	29	1	16.7
in New Zealand	18	3	15	0	16.7
in Australia	18	3	14	1	16.7

2011 Springbok Rugby World Cup Squad

Forwards

Willem Alberts, Bakkies Botha, Heinrich Brüssow, Schalk Burger, Bismarck du Plessis, Jannie du Plessis, Francois Louw, Victor Matfield (vc), Tendai Mtawarira, Johann Muller, Chiliboy Ralepelle, Danie Rossouw, John Smit (c), Pierre Spies, Gurthrö Steenkamp, CJ van der Linde.

Backs

Gio Aplon, Juan de Jongh, Jean de Villiers, Fourie du Preez, Jaque Fourie, Bryan Habana, Francois Hougaard, Butch James, Pat Lambie, Odwa Ndungane, Ruan Pienaar, JP Pietersen, Francois Steyn, Morné Steyn.

Management

Peter de Villiers (head coach), Gary Gold (assistant coach), Dick Muir (assistant coach), Percy Montgomery (kicking coach), Jacques Nienaber (defence coach/physiotherapist), Malome Maimane (technical analyst), Rassie Erasmus (technical specialist), Neels Liebel (conditioning coach), Dr Derik Coetzee (conditioning coach), Dr Craig Roberts (team doctor), Rene Naylor (physiotherapist), Vivian Verwant (physiotherapist), Daliah Hurwitz (massage therapist), Charles Wessels (logistics manager), Mkiti Malakoane (baggage master), AnneLee Murray (PR manager), Andy Colquhoun (media manager).

Selected Player Profiles (to end 2012)

Jean de Villiers

Height: 190cm

Weight: 100kg

Springbok caps: 84

Tries: 20

Total points: 100

Honours: SA Rugby Player of the Year nominee (2005); SA Rugby Player of the Year (2008); Players' Player of the Year (2008)

Holds record for most capped Springbok centre (69 in this position)

Shares record for most Tests as Springbok centre combination with Jaque Fourie (26)

Jan Nathaniel du Plessis

Height: 188cm

Weight: 120kg

Springbok caps: 42

Tries: 1

Total points: 5

Holds record for most Springbok Tests played with a brother: Bismarck (24)

Bismarck Wilhelm du Plessis

Height: 189cm
Weight: 113kg
Springbok caps: 46
Tries: 6
Total points: 30
Honours: SA Player of the Year nominee (2008 and 2011)
Holds the record for Test tries scored by a Springbok hooker (6)

Schalk Willem Petrus Burger

Height: 193cm
Weight: 110kg
Springbok caps: 68
Tries: 13
Total points: 65
Honours: SA Rugby Player of the Year (2004 and 2011); Young
    SA Rugby Player of the Year nominee (2003 and 2004): IRB
    Player of the Year (2004)
Along with Juan Smith, holds the record for most tries scored
    in Tests by a Springbok flank (11) and is the most capped
    Springbok flank ever

Sources

Books

De Villiers, Peter, with Gavin Rich. *Politically Incorrect: The Autobiography*. Cape Town: Zebra Press, 2012.

Du Preez, Max. *Louis Luyt Unauthorised*. Cape Town: Zebra Press, 2001.

Gladwell, Malcolm. *Outliers*. New York: Little Brown, 2008.

Grieb, Eddie and Duane Heath. *South African Rugby Annual 2013*. Cape Town: South African Rugby, 2011.

Keohane, Mark. *Springbok Rugby Uncovered*. Cape Town: Zebra Press, 2004.

Luyt, Louis. *Walking Proud: The Louis Luyt Autobiography*. Cape Town: Don Nelson, 2004.

Matfield, Victor, with De Jongh Borchardt. *Victor: My Journey*. Cape Town: Zebra Press, 2011.

Pain, Dr Matt TG and Pain, Matthew A. 'Essay: Risk taking in sport'. *The Lancet*, Volume 366, 1 December 2005.

Smit, John, with Mike Greenaway. *Captain in the Cauldron*. Cape Town: Highbury Safika Media, 2009.

Van der Valk, Rob, with Andy Colquhoun. *Nick & I: An Adventure in Rugby*. Cape Town: Don Nelson, 2002.

White, Jake, with Craig Ray. *In Black and White: The Jake White Story*. Cape Town: Zebra Press, 2007.

Archives
UWC-Robben Island Mayibuye Archives

Websites
www.genslin.us/bokkke/sarugby.html
www.srsa.gov.za
www.sarugby.co.za
www.rugby.com.au
www.rugby365.com
www.keo.co.za
www.nzru.co.nz
www.aru
www.sarugby.co.za
www.naspers.co.za

Newspapers
Business Day
Cape Times
Cape Argus
Rapport
Sunday Times
The Times
Beeld

Acknowledgements

By the time one reaches the final stages of the researching, writing and producing of a book, it feels more like a team effort than a solitary one. I'm particularly grateful to Jonathan Ball publishing director Jeremy Boraine, who has stood by me through every twist and turn this book has taken. Writer and rugby coach John Dobson read the entire manuscript and gave invaluable feedback. Every intervention in the text by super-sharp editor Alfred LeMaitre greatly improved it. Thanks to everyone at Jonathan Ball, a highly professional team and a pleasure to work with.

I'm also indebted to the following, for various reasons, and in no particular order: Andrew and Guy McGregor, Margaret Hoffman, Sarah Nuttall, Archie Henderson, Barbara Erasmus, Peter Church, Barend van Graan, Sister Francis, Louis de Villiers, Stephen Nell, Russell Belter, Xola Ntshinga, Gavin Rich, Liam del Carme, Craig Ray, Mike Greenaway, Brenden Nel, Zeena Isaacs, Vata Ngobeni, Andy Colquhoun, De Jongh Borchardt, Nick Mallett, Paul Dobson, Rob van der Valk, Tim Noakes, Howard Kahn, Wally Mason, Max du Preez, Irma du Plessis and Andries Bezuidenhout.